# Late Have I Loved Thee

## BOOKS BY SUSAN MUTO

*Approaching the Sacred: An Introduction to Spiritual Reading*

*Blessings That Make Us Be:*
*A Formative Approach to Living the Beatitudes*

*Celebrating the Single Life: A Spirituality for*
*Single Persons in Today's World*

*John of the Cross for Today: The Ascent*

*John of the Cross for Today: The Dark Night*

*The Journey Homeward: On the Road to Spiritual Reading*

*Meditation in Motion*

*Pathways of Spiritual Living*

*A Practical Guide to Spiritual Reading*

*Renewed at Each Awakening:*
*The Formative Power of Sacred Words*

*Steps along the Way: The Path of Spiritual Reading*

*Womanspirit: Reclaiming the*
*Deep Feminine in Our Human Spirituality*

## WITH ADRIAN VAN KAAM

*Aging Gracefully*

*Am I Living a Spiritual Life?*

*Commitment: Key to Christian Maturity*

*Commitment: Key to Christian Maturity, A Workbook and Guide*

*Divine Guidance: Seeking to Find and Follow the Will of God*

*Formation Guide to Becoming Spiritually Mature*

*Harnessing Stress: A Spiritual Quest*

*Healthy and Holy under Stress: A Royal Road to Wise Living*

*The Participant Self*

*Power of Appreciation: A New Approach to Personal*
*and Relational Healing*

*Practicing the Prayer of Presence*

*Songs for Every Season*

*Stress and the Search for Happiness: A New Challenge*
*for Christian Spirituality*

# Late Have
# I Loved Thee

## *The Recovery
of Intimacy*

## Susan Muto

CROSSROAD • NEW YORK

1995
The Crossroad Publishing Company
370 Lexington Avenue, New York, NY 10017

"Living in Everyday Intimacy," a twelve-part series by
Susan Muto, Ph.D., was originally published in the January
through December, 1994 issues of *Liguorian* magazine.

**Library of Congress Cataloging-in-Publication Data**

Muto, Susan Annette.
     Late have I loved thee : the recovery of intimacy /
Susan Muto.
          p.   cm.
     Includes bibliographical references.
     ISBN 0-8245-1545-5; 0-8245-1522-6 (pbk.)
     1. Intimacy (Psychology)—Religious aspects—
Christianity. 2. Spiritual life—Catholic Church. 3.
Catholic Church—Doctrines.
I. Title.
BV4597.53.I55M88   1995
248.4—dc20                                      95-19255
                                                CIP

To my friends and colleagues
at the Epiphany Association,
I dedicate this book
with love and gratitude
for our intimacy in the Lord.

# ❦ Contents ❧

Late have I loved Thee, O
beauty so ancient and so new, late
have I loved Thee! And behold,
Thou wert within and I was without. I was looking for Thee out
there, and I threw myself, deformed
as I was, upon those well-formed
things which Thou hast made.
Thou wert with me, yet I was not
with Thee. These things held me
far from Thee, things which would
not have existed had they not been
in Thee. Thou didst call and cry
out and burst in upon my deafness;
Thou didst shine forth and glow
and drive away my blindness; Thou
didst send forth Thy fragrance, and
I drew in my breath, and now I
pant for Thee; I have tasted, and
now I hunger and thirst; Thou
didst touch me, and I was inflamed
with desire for Thy peace.
— *St. Augustine*

# Introduction

Without intimacy we cannot exist humanly. Its recovery has to be the shared goal of humanity.

Infants deprived of a warm parental touch die early. With enough love from good caregivers they may survive, but it is not easy. God knows, it is never too late for someone to see the real me.

Love is like an epiphany. It has the power to change things. So does intimacy. Its everyday recovery moves us from distrust to trust, from fear to faith, from self-enclosure to mutual disclosure.

St. Augustine found the true source of "beauty so ancient and so new" after much agonized soul-searching. His *Confessions* are a classic example of the recovery of intimacy. When he remembered in honestly painful detail the events of his infancy, youth, and adulthood, he had to admit that God was not "out there" but "with me." How he regretted not loving totally the God who was all the while within, loving him. Long had he awaited the gift of recovered intimacy. Thanks to divine grace, it was not too late. In repentance and prayer of the heart, with much laughter and tears, Augustine experienced anew his intimate interconnection with God, self, and others.

I have written this book to show that in a climate of individualism where suspicion and mistrust fill the air, the gift of intimacy lets us see into our shared humanity. Work overload, violent streets, and broken relationships might kill intimacy were it not for our capacity to echo Augustine's passionate cry for love and peace—a cry that pierced the heavens.

What we crave are not occasional thrills, like the temporary effects of an emotional high or the heady feeling of a successful business deal, but the grace of steady, everyday intimacy. We find it in a warm hug after a hard day, in the trusting smile we exchange over a cup of coffee, or in the meeting of minds and hearts with good friends.

Intimacy is an overall feeling of well-being that greets us on a sunny day when all seems right with the world.

If the truth were told, what we really long for is a sense of oneness, of union and communion, with the Divine Forming Mystery we call God. As believers, we want that inner liberation from sin and death only Jesus can give to us. He is our door to intimacy with God, others, and self. To emulate his hidden life is to celebrate everyday work and play. It is to labor for a higher purpose to the degree that what we do becomes an expression of who we are.

When we enjoy God's nearness, prayer is like play. Ours is a relationship of carefree abandonment to a beneficial mystery. It is as if God bounces us in the air like children laughing. Worry wanes. Fear fades. Joy abounds. Peace prevails. We humans become fully alive. Such is the grace of recovered intimacy.

Like a detective writing a mystery story, I have been tracing this theme for quite some time. It began with a book I first wrote in 1982 entitled *Celebrating the Single*

# ❧ INTRODUCTION ❧

*Life: A Spirituality for Single Persons in Today's World.* The search continued in my more autobiographical books, *Meditation in Motion* (1986) and *Womanspirit: Reclaiming the Deep Feminine in Our Human Spirituality* (1992).

To be free to just *be*, to reclaim the deepest truths of our shared faith and formation tradition, and to trust our story, became life-themes in these books. That is why I accepted to write a year-long series for the *Liguorian* magazine on intimacy (from January to December, 1994). This book represents the culmination of these endeavors.

I want to thank at the start Fr. Allen Weinert, editor of *Liguorian*, for inviting me to write the series, and Michael Leach, my editor and publisher at Crossroad, for expressing interest in the book-length version. My colleague and mentor, Fr. Adrian van Kaam, C.S.Sp., Ph.D., never wavered in his support, seeing "formative intimacy" as an essential component of Christian spirituality. Thanks are also in order for the tireless help I received in manuscript preparation from Marilyn Russell, our administrative assistant, and from Mary Lou Perez, our secretary, whose help in redrafting the text was in itself an example of celebrating everyday work properly balanced by playful togetherness.

For me this book was in a special way a labor of love. I'm happy to say that writing it was also play—a play convincing me that the recovery of intimacy ought to be the goal of our age, and the hope of the next century.

# ❧ 1 ❧

# Three Avenues to Everyday Intimacy

TO LIVE IN THE PAST AND THE FUTURE IS EASY.
TO LIVE IN THE PRESENT IS LIKE THREADING A NEEDLE.

—Walker Percy

I once heard a funny story that makes a serious point. A person showing signs of depression decided to go to confession. What was weighing heavily on her took a while to express, but finally she blurted out to her priest: "Bless me, Father, for I have sinned. I do not have an intimate friend!"

True or not, the confession is suggestive. Many popular books seem to say that we are nowhere without soul-mates, private spiritual directors, or shared faith groups. Granted, these special relationships and sessions can be powerful aids along the way to faith deepening. The question is, whatever happened to ordinary, unspectacular everyday-ness—like the thirty years Jesus spent in his hometown of Nazareth? It was such a "nothing" existence that it did not merit more than a sentence or two in the New Testament. Yet it was here that the bulk of the Lord's own spiritual formation took place. His everyday life became epiphanic—radiant with deeper meaning—and so must ours.

How do we live in ordinary intimacy with the people, events, and things that enter our world both expectantly and unexpectantly?

Let me clarify something from the start. Whether you are male or female, young or old, single or married, believer or non-believer, neither you nor any human being on the face of the Earth can survive as distinctively human without receiving and giving the gift of ordinary intimacy. This common way of contact connects us with one another in tears and laughter, in sorrow and joy.

The faces of intimacy are as diverse as stars, as unique as snowflakes. Pick up any book of portraits, any record of history, and you will see what I mean. Walk through any park on a summer's day and catch a couple in love smiling into each others' eyes. Stop by a hospital room and observe the way a compassionate nurse bathes the fevered brow of a sick child. See how a mechanic touches with pride the car he has repaired, and you'll see another sign of recovered intimacy. It happens to us when we really trust another person, when we receive selfless love, and when we take care of things like good stewards do.

Do you think intimacy is beyond you? Then try to recall a festivity with family members, a pleasant conversation with old friends, the soft touch of a lamb's wool scarf protecting your neck from cold weather. These are all good examples of everyday intimacy.

These times of togetherness around events, people, and things are woven into the fabric of daily life. All

three offer common access points to peaceful, non-posses-
sive intimacy; they are freely given and freely received.

Sadly, in our era we have come to associate "intimacy"
or "being intimate with someone" with genital-sexual
expression—as if physical intimacy were the only way to
find relief from loneliness and to feel love. The urge for
this kind of intimacy makes people, especially when they
are young and restless, oblivious to the many ways in
which "I" want another or others to "see into me," an
interesting play on the word "intimacy."

I believe we must recover the art and discipline of letting ordinary events, persons, and things invite us to see
into their deepest meaning. Let me illustrate what I'm
trying to say with an example.

I have an unforgettable memory of recovered intimacy in my own life. It happened many years ago when I
visited the Pope John XXIII Center in the Bronx near
Fordham University to see a priest whose writings I had
long taught and admired. Fr. Walter Ciszek, S.J. was a
saintly spiritual guide and an incredibly brave soul for
whose beatification I now pray.

At the time of our visit, Father had recently returned to
the United States after years of imprisonment behind the
Iron Curtain. As he records in his inspiring books, *With God
in Russia* and *He Leadeth Me*, those were the years when he
learned what it meant to listen to the will of God not "out
there" but in one's here-and-now life situation.

I will never forget how his countenance lit up with
the peace and joy of the Lord when he greeted me on this
midweek evening and welcomed me to the center. I
arrived very late, but bright and early the next morning I
heard a knock on my door. To my delight, it was Father

Walter himself, asking me if I wanted to join him in the chapel for Mass. Because of the timing of my visit no other guests were there. It was only the two of us. I felt as if a veil between earth and heaven had been lifted—so lovely was the Eastern rite service over which he presided.

Afterwards he came over to the pew where I was in prayer and asked me politely if I would like some breakfast. Could he cook for me? I could hardly believe my ears. It was as if the Lord himself were inviting me into the kitchen.

I cannot recall much of what we said. All I knew was that I found myself in the presence of a person who was God's intimate. He asked me in utter simplicity how I wanted my eggs. I answered, as if it were an everyday occurrence to be served by a saint, "Over lightly." When he placed the dish before me—the eggs cooked to perfection—I had a sudden urge to preserve them in wax like a first-class relic.

Slowly, over two cups of coffee, in the most simple exchanges of life's ups and downs, I had the sensation of being with someone who could read my soul. We enjoyed the blissful gift of ordinary intimacy.

To this day that encounter in the kitchen stands out as a time when I was touched by the finger of God. I felt confirmed by his messenger to follow my vocation as a single Christian in the world.

In and through life's comings and goings we are meant to sense the sustaining hand of the Father, the tender warmth of the Son, the peaceful rest of the Holy Spirit. I cannot find words to capture the simple yet profound exchange of everyday intimacy I enjoyed for a brief duration with a true spiritual friend.

4

Is there a way to walk this path on a regular basis? How can we avoid cheap substitutes for true transcendent encounter, for the kind of bonding that goes beyond or more deeply into who we are called to be?

Is there a time-tested pattern by which we can build bridges of grace between ourselves and others, bridges by which we can cross hand in hand over to the God who made us and keeps us and all events and things in being?

I believe such a pattern can be found in our Christian faith and formation tradition. It takes the form of three intersecting avenues to the recovery of intimacy that I call listening attentively, loving respectfully, and living simply.

In traditional language, these are the three evangelical counsels of obedience, chastity, and poverty, known also as the three vows. Adrian van Kaam refers to these as constituting the threefold path.[1] In them we find general directions for achieving oneness with the Trinity and new-found nearness to the events, people, and things that comprise our daily life.[2] These classical counsels become trustworthy guides to everyday intimacy.

## OBEDIENCE: SEEING INTO EVENTS

Going to the Center to meet Father Walter turned out to be an event that made a strong impression on me. It was an ordinary happening that enabled me to see something that was "more than" I expected, something extraordinary. I came away a better person. Father Walter taught me both by example and by words to listen respectfully to the still, small voice of the Spirit at the core of my being, as well as in every event of my daily life.

To listen in this way is to hear or "obey " (*ob-audire*) the graced direction offered to us by the Most High in the most near, for instance, in a neighbor who needs to talk to me as much as I needed to talk to Father Walter.

It is not easy to listen to events as disclosures of intimacy, to pay attention to their deeper meaning. Instead of judging others harshly, jumping to conclusions, or refusing to let them say their piece, we try to attend to the forming presence of God in every situation. Instead of swallowing our morning coffee in one quick gulp, we pause long enough to thank God for the beginning of a new day and to savor its flavor.

> *Being present to every event—from a meal on the table to a revealing meditation—is an excellent way to foster the recovery of everyday intimacy.*

The invitation to see into events as sent to us by the Transcendent comes many times during each working day. Do we hear it? Are we obedient to it? Or are we too busy?

To be intimate with Jesus or anyone else for that matter, we must still the noise within us. Then we can be more alert to all that surrounds us. We live in a posture of surrender to the providential meaning of each event rather than being caught in the net of our own narrow expectations.

The events of daily life, when seen from a faith perspective, become invitations, challenges, and appeals from the Holy Spirit to our human spirit. A chance meeting between strangers on a plane may invite a sharing more intimate than one enjoys with a parent or a spouse. A discriminatory situation at work may challenge us to call for a change in management. The plight of a family on welfare may appeal to our charity while promoting a reexamination of our own spending habits. Any event can lead to deeper listening if we remain on intimate terms with our Divine Director.

It helps to remember that by virtue of our baptism we share in the obedience of Jesus to the Father, in his "Yes" to life as a salvation event. Every time we listen to events—from awakening in the morning to retiring at night—as pointers to the Transcendent, we walk with Jesus on the highways and byways of ordinary intimacy. Suddenly we start to appreciate every event as an epiphany of the Mystery: a loaf of bread, a glass of wine, a friendly face, an awesome storm, a radiant rainbow.

> *Our personal intimacy with Christ blends with a felt sense of his presence in the events that make up our seemingly uneventful days.*

Obedience prompts us to listen to more than just the practical details of work and play. We are able to be present to whatever is happening as a providential pointer to God's loving and allowing will in our lives.

Intimacy, thus understood, reconnects every event or branch on the tree of our life to the vine that is Christ. We see the temporal as a pointer to the eternal. Our ears are more open to others, our arms more receptive. We become more prone to address their needs. We are led by the Spirit, step by step, to the next facet of recovered intimacy—loving people respectfully and chastely.

## CHASTITY: SEEING INTO PEOPLE

While Father Walter cooked my breakfast, I watched him moving around the kitchen with the wonder of a child.

Having been confined to prison for so long, he was denied this ordinary pleasure. He approached each task—from cracking the eggs to setting the table—with child-like wonder. Unlike most of us, he had not lost the ability to enjoy the intimate contacts and connections everyone needs. How shocked he would have been by the loss of respect we witness everywhere. Gross evidence of the near demise of chaste love can be seen in the rise of domestic violence, the plague of abuse, the eruption of religious wars, the wanton slaughter of the innocent.

More subtle forms of disrespect affect us when someone insults us with a mean look or a cutting remark, or expects more of us than we can give. A young woman's bid for ordinary intimacy may be shunned or misinterpreted by a man who only wants "sex" severed from committed marital love. It seems harder and harder for the young to follow high moral standards.

What happens to intimacy in this climate of unchaste, disrespectful relations? What does it take to reform this abusive atmosphere?

Reformation happens when we remember who we are and what we are called to do. Father Walter spent several years recalling what he had learned from his spiritual mentors about loving and living God's will in everydayness. During years of enforced solitude, he understood anew the cumulative wisdom of his faith community.

Our life, too, from infancy to old age, is an invitation to relationship. We cannot mature without the care and companionship of others. They show us in ordinary and dramatic ways the love God bestows on us at every moment.

To become givers as well as receivers of ordinary intimacy, our love has to be purified of self-gratifying passions that make others the objects of our pleasure. We also have to chasten our needy, overdependent demands for acclaim and attention. One of the reasons it was great to be with Father Walter was that he had no idea of what a superb spiritual guide he was. His humility created space for chaste love.

Respectful loving does not have strings attached. We treat with compassion the people Holy Providence places on our path. A parishioner in the pew extends a hand in peace and we shake it warmly. A blind stranger takes our arm and we cross the street together as old friends might do. A passenger on a plane asks if we can change seats because the window side frightens her and we politely oblige.

Encounters such as these are life-giving. They supplement the more intense forms of intimacy we enjoy with close friends and family members. They help us to see into ourselves as we are seen by others. What we respect is our mutual God-given dignity. Father Walter made me feel what I believed: we are all members of Christ's mystical Body, participants in the life of the Trinity. Though sinners, we belong to the communion of saints.

The task before us is not an easy one. We have to try to love people chastely and respectfully in an abusive, pornographic climate. I cannot do this alone and neither can you. We need Christ in our life to help us move from selfish sensuality to self-giving intimacy.

## POVERTY: SEEING INTO THINGS

I never thought a plate of over-lightly eggs would mean so much to me, but this simple meal spoke to me of Father Walter's spirit of simplicity and poverty. I saw in his gentle

9

demeanor a Christ figure detached from possessions as ultimate, yet seeing all creation as good. The things he owned were gifts of God. In cooked eggs he helped me to see something of our Creator's care.

More and more I think that the recovery of intimacy goes together with at least some simplification of life. Having too many things takes up too much of our time. To live simply means to detach ourselves from the holding power of possessions. Have you ever watched the faces of people in a casino? It looks as if they believe their lives depend on winning. They are captives of consumerism, whether they know it or not. What would it take to remind them that things like poker chips are not ends in themselves? Try telling this to a person addicted to gambling or drugs or alcohol. It takes hitting bottom for them to admit their ultimate dependency on God.

I have become conscious lately of the need to simplify my life—not to add to its quantity, but to its quality. I want to enjoy the inner freedom and intimacy poverty of spirit brings. I was not born to shop, but to see God (cf. Matt. 5:1).

Edified by the reverent way he celebrated the Eucharist that morning, I knew Father Walter enjoyed the grace of intimacy with the Trinity. He emulated Christ by his life of love and service. He was poor by worldly standards but rich in the virtues of social justice, peace, and mercy.

To see *simply* is to behold things as gifts of God. We are not their owners but their stewards and protectors. We keep sight of the whole picture rather than riveting on any limited part of it as if it were ultimate. In the poverty of a prison cell, Walter Ciszek found more inner freedom and intimacy with things than we who are rich by comparison often do. He and the other prisoners treasured the smallest thing, such as a crust of bread, as a gift of great worth.

I once met members of an African village in Tanzania, who cared for one another with more profound affection than I saw among the parishioners in my church. Everyone knew one another by name. Their lives were as simple as their commitment to life was profound.

Without poverty of spirit, we cannot touch things lovingly—as the people of the village did their cooking utensils and the homemade gifts they gave me. We begin to use and abuse objects in culture and nature as if we owned them. Is this why people show so little ecological sensitivity? Until we become content with less, we cannot stop raping our land. Lacking detachment, we lose track of the truth that we possess nothing.

A friend recently asked me if our Epiphany Association could make use of a collection of clothing from an estate he was closing. I felt happy for the poor who could use these garments. Yet I could not suppress the wave of pity I felt for the lady who needed fifty pairs of suede shoes.

Living simply prevents us from behaving with careless indifference toward others in need. We feel a bond of kinship between us and every creature under the sun. We enjoy the ebb and flow typical of ordinary intimacy—being attached to things as gifts while being detached from them as ultimate. Poverty of spirit enables us to treat things reverently, to see into their deepest form and meaning. We go beyond their outer appearance to the inner mystery they conceal.

To acknowledge our all-too-human poverty is at the same time to proclaim our spiritual wealth. Poverty of spirit points to our hunger and thirst for intimate union with the Trinity. We thank God for the loveliness of things while being mindful of their limits. Nothing on earth can make us totally happy when we glimpse in faith the world awaiting us above the stars.

By following these three avenues to recovered intimacy, we grow in wisdom and peace of heart. Obedience helps us to overcome the blindness of inattention and to listen appreciatively to all sides of our life situation. In the many voices calling us through everyday events, we hear the one voice we hold most dear.

Chaste loving heals the fractured relations that hurt people when sin prevails over virtue, when division replaces respect for diversity, when indifference triumphs over our longing for intimacy.

Living simply in poverty of spirit enables us to let go of things as final sources of satisfaction. Then we can see them as gifts given by God to draw us closer to the divine wellspring from whence the "late have I loved Thee" of ordinary intimacy flows abundantly.

1. See Adrian van Kaam, *The Vowed Life* (Denville, N.J.: Dimension Books, 1968).

2. See Susan Muto and Adrian van Kaam, *Commitment: Key to Christian Maturity* (Mahwah, N.J.: Paulist Press, 1989), 25–58; and Susan Muto and Adrian van Kaam, *Commitment: Key to Christian Maturity, a Workbook and Guide* (Mahwah, N.J.: Paulist Press, 1991), 51–80.

Blessed Trinity,
Unity in diversity,
Epitome of intimacy,
Grant me the grace to see
Life as an epiphany of your mystery,
Events as pointers to a sustaining hand,
People as belonging to the same Promised Land,
Things as gifts of love's own spirit.
May everyday life be
A reminder that we
Are all branches
Of the Vine Divine,
Never alone,
Only on the way home.

# ❧ 2 ❧

# Befriending One Another—
# The Gateway to
# Recovering Intimacy

THE TRUTH OF LIFE IS THAT LOVE IS A GIFT,
THAT RELATIONSHIPS ARE COMMITMENTS,
THAT SEXUALITY IS A SACRAMENT OF SPIRITUALITY.

—Eugene H. Peterson

"Do we really need to know more about the rise of sexually transmitted diseases, the epidemic levels of infidelity, the systematic destruction of family life?" So asked a single friend of mine. She, like the other guests who gathered for coffee and conversation in my living room, said she was tired of hearing nothing but bad news. Everyone nodded in consent. I asked as the evening progressed, "Is the enjoyment of everyday intimacy a possibility or an impossible dream?"

Another friend, the mother of two teenage boys, chose not to reply directly to the question. Instead she shared her concerns with us: "Will the boys be able to resist the push and pull of peer pressure? I think it promotes a near addiction to uncommitted, premarital sex. Why do so many kids buy into empty promises of happiness?"

We all agreed that fly-by-night relationships can never fulfill a person's need for loving, responsible nearness. Whether one is married or single, one needs committed caring friends. The more we thought about it, the more it seemed to us that friendship itself might be the answer to educating our population to the joys of ordinary intimacy.

I want to identify first what hinders this gift. Next I'd like to consider what helps us to find and foster the friendship Jesus himself offers us (cf. John 15:15).

## STUMBLING BLOCKS TO BEFRIENDING OTHERS

Real intimacy seeks deeper commitment. Romantic love shuns it. What blocks committed love in the lives of many single people is a slow slide into an exhausting cycle of "seduce and conquer." Life becomes a terrible loneliness.

A pseudo-form of intimacy, bound to sensual experiences, may imprison a person's mind, heart, and spirit. Pretending to be liberated, one is really a prisoner of needs that are never satisfied. Going from one form of physical gratification to another becomes as entrapping as any addiction. A lonely person compulsively seeking instant intimacy quickly enters a dead-end street.

Sex without love, irresponsible lack of commitment, and sheer loneliness are stubborn stumbling blocks to the recovery of intimacy. But no obstacle is more prevalent in our time than the loss of genuine spiritual friendship. For persons addicted to quick-fix gratification, gentle, honorable, honest friendships between members of the same or the opposite sex are, sad to say, a distant dream.

Many transcendent desires are frustrated by lower level attachments that leave one feeling empty and demeaned. What must it be like to awaken in the morning wavering on the edge of despair? In what way might recovered intimacy in the form of spiritual friendship reverse this predicament?

What makes befriending another for his or her own sake such a joy is that this relationship is always oriented toward inclusivity rather than exclusivity. Trustworthy intimacy of this sort widens one's circle of loving; it avoids fixating on any one person to such a degree that no other evokes feelings of affinity and friendly appreciation.

The opposite of spiritual friendship is encapsulation. Nothing curtails our freedom to be and become who we are more than manipulative or seductive relationships. It is a betrayal of friendship to gain power over others or to treat them as *our* possessions.

Dispositions of dominance and submission destroy trust. They breed abusive behavior to such a degree that people who are victims tend to resist the very intimacy they need for healing. Having never known the respectful love of spiritual friendship, they may only be able to escape the harsher side of life in empty pleasure-seeking or by themselves becoming perpetrators of the abuse they endured.

When the grace of spiritual friendship is absent or unknown, people may deny their intimacy needs altogether. They become cynical, sarcastic, condescending, or simply afraid to let others near them. Some develop a veneer of superficial give-and-take. Others don an indifferent mask to make sure the last laugh is not on them.

To dismiss the efficacy of normal intimacy does not make the longing for closeness to others and to the Divine Other disappear. Under the guise of nonchalance, there often lurks a person who feels worthless. Compensatory anger replaces a longing for gentle love. One's outlook on life is bleak, sour, resentful. What good is life when self-pity and low-grade depression replace peace and joy? Life begins to feel like a useless burden one has to carry alone. Relief seems to be a galaxy away. At what may well be the breaking point, humanly speaking, one may find that a major conversion of heart is on the verge of breaking through.

## THE WAY TO GROW IN INTIMACY

Jesus' exact words in the Gospel of John are: "I no longer speak of you as slaves. . . . Instead, I call you friends" (John 15:15). He also asks us to "love one another as I have loved you" (John 15:12).

This will to love is the essence of trustworthy intimacy. Without this deep inner commitment to befriend God and others with loving solicitude, the world becomes a sad and lonely place.

As Christians who follow the way of love, we are further called "to go forth and bear fruit" (John 15:16). We are not alone. We belong to one and the same family of faith. All must follow the command to be lovers as Jesus was. Friendship with him is thus the foundation of true spiritual friendship for others.

Jesus promises that "Where two or three are gathered in my name, there am I in their midst" (Matt. 18:20).

*17*

When friends of Christ come together for sharing, laughter, discourse, and healthy debate, he is with us. An aura of mutual respect for each one's dignity helps people who were once strangers to be open and honest with one another. By our words and our presence we show support for each other's life call. Young and old, single or married, female or male, we become a community of faith enjoying the grace of spiritual friendship, for, in the words of Antoine de Saint-Exupéry: "Love does not consist in gazing at each other but in looking outward together in the same direction."[1]

If we direct our eyes toward Jesus, we cannot be hurtful to one another. In a spirit-filled atmosphere of mutual trust and care, fraternal correction can be as healing as honest conversation. There is no room in real relationships for intimacy-deflating patterns of domination and submission. The will to love others in the Lord precludes possessiveness or crass put-downs.

The German poet Rilke wrote that in the state of friendship there is space and freedom for growth. Such a love, Rilke said, consists in this: "that two solitudes protect and touch and greet each other."[2]

Being together in trustworthy intimacy teaches us to reappreciate the little things that make life great. How happy we are to speak from the heart and feel that we are really understood, to be ourselves without having to prove anything. The relaxation we need is enhanced by this atmosphere of mutual acceptance. We can let down our hair, as the expression goes, with no need to hide our vulnerability.

In the presence of friends who freely share their love for the Lord, we experience being drawn by grace into prayers of thanksgiving and genuine peace.

Recovered intimacy is not only a gift of the Spirit; it is also an excellent stress-reducer. People long for this kind of mutuality. We all know on some level that nothing can replace the give-and-take of true friendship lived within the context of a solid faith and formation tradition.

## SOME FRUITS OF SPIRITUAL FRIENDSHIP

No matter how terrible my day has been, if I can talk it over with a friend who understands me, I always feel better. Because we have passed the test of trust, we do not have to fear terrible things like envy or betrayal. The opposite is also true: high stress happens to people when they are with their immediate family or in the workplace more than anywhere else. Places that ought to be safe havens for ordinary intimacy are arenas of inner warfare and worry.

What a relief it is to communicate with someone who puts our best interests first. I have a friend who helps me through the pain of self-reflection without pushing too hard. I feel at ease asking for her advice, because I know her response to my plight will be both caring and challenging.

Good friends are safe sounding boards: they can help us avoid making serious mistakes, and they have an uncanny ability to sense when we need company and when we need to be alone. Mulling over serious matters can be as engaging as taking time for sheer fun.

The gifts I receive from my friends do not necessarily come in ribboned boxes. The best things they give me are new insights or needed critiques. Without trusted others in my life, to whom would I turn with my hopes and concerns?

I know from experience that without a solid shoulder to lean on I soon become nervous and tense. Who but a friend would never manipulate or misdirect me?

Spiritual friendship is not an end in itself; it leads to growth in intimacy with others and God. It surrounds us like the air we breathe, giving us the confidence we need to carry on. My friends remind me in so many words that when the going gets tough, the tough get going. Together we dare to ask if we are in tune with the Lord or if our own willfulness is standing in the way of his leadership.

Christian friendship attunes us to the Spirit. It opens us to the Mystery of transforming love that goes beyond self-centered agendas. We sense what it means to care for others as we are cared for by God with untiring generosity.

It always seems as if our conversation has reached a high plateau when we tell each other the story of our faith, hope, and love in God. We know that the love we feel for one another in the Lord is like the glue that holds together the integrity of our relationship. Our belief in the healing, forgiving friendship of Jesus is the key to recovered intimacy.

Those few special relationships we call irreplaceable are like lifelines. They bail us out of stormy seas. They are of greater worth than gold.

That is why the death of good friends is a loss from which one never fully recovers. Mourning does not diminish how much we miss them. After my father died, when people called to console my mother, I heard her say again and again, "I've lost my best friend."

Sharing at such a deep level is not without risk. Trial and error test friendship. Who of us has not been hurt once or twice by trusting too quickly?

Intimacy pushed away or betrayed ought not to result in our withdrawing to a safety zone of non-involvement. Neither should we settle for the bargain-basement variety of friendship that says, in effect, "I'll love you only if you do this or that to please me."

If our love has too many strings attached, we may never savor the delights of ordinary intimacy. A friendship lacking any semblance of freedom of spirit and unconditional love may either die quickly or slowly become unstitched. We begin to see that what we thought of as friendship was merely a fair-weather encounter. Perhaps we build up expectations another can never fulfill. When the shaky bridge between us crumbles, we feel forlorn. Who is to blame? More often than not, we refused to read the signs posted along the way.

Not every relationship we enter into can last. Lifelong friendships are among life's rarest gems. In the words of the fourteenth-century Cistercian abbot Aelred of Rievaulx:

> Friendship . . . is that virtue by which spirits are bound by ties of love and sweetness, and out of many are made one. Even the philosophers of this world have ranked friendship not with things casual or transitory but with the virtues which are eternal."[3]

What sets a friendship on course is the joy we feel in one another's company and in the way our love as committed Christians models the loving communion of the Holy Trinity. The ordinary intimacy we cherish in and through the gift of spiritual friendship is but a dim reflection of the divine intimacy we are destined to enjoy eternally in God.

Friendship is the gateway to recovering intimacy. It branches into the smoothly paved roads of self-donation, mutuality, trust, and reciprocity. Together we become little words in the Divine Word.

In the light of the Trinity, we see that the way of salvation is not a lonely walk accomplished by individualistic will power. Rather, it is a venture taken in reciprocal care and concern. As a friend, paraphrasing Jesus (cf. John 13:25), told me, "This is how people will know we take our faith seriously—by the love that keeps our feet on the ground and our eyes on the stars."

1. Quoted in Anne Morrow Lindberg, *Gift from the Sea* (New York: Pantheon Books, 1955), 81.
2. Ibid., 94.
3. Aelred of Rievaulx, *On Spiritual Friendship*, trans. Mary Eugenia Laker (Washington, D.C.: Cistercian Publications, 1974), 55.

Holy Trinity,
Mystery of loving communion,
Invitation to deeper union.
Grant me the grace to pass
The test of trust.
Teach me to be self-donating,
To express freely
A commitment to mutuality,
To ever loving,
Quietly befriending reciprocity.
Strengthen my will to love
My sisters and brothers
As you love us and all others.

# ❦ 3 ❦

# The Ordinary Seen as Extraordinary through Intimate Eyes

A CHILD'S QUITE TOUCHING EPIPHANY: SEEING
PRAYER AND THE SEARCH FOR GOD NOT AS A
FLEETING VISION, ISOLATED FROM THE EVENTS OF THIS
WORLD, BUT AS A MEANS OF CONNECTING ONESELF
TO THE ORDINARY MOMENTS OF LIVING.

—Robert Coles

People of all faiths love St. Francis of Assisi because he was a seer. For him every moment of life was an invitation to intimacy with God, others, self, and the whole created world. Routines that most saw as pointless and boring—like brick laying in a brokendown church—assumed for him a radiance beyond all telling.

Francis, like the spiritual masters of many traditions, knew how important it was to develop the disposition of concentrated awareness. Simply put, this means to see into the ordinary as extraordinary.[1] As we clear our "monkey minds" of myriad distractions, as we learn to pay attention and avoid dissipation, what we see may surprise us.

I awaken on an average weekday morning. I rise, shower, dress, and prepare breakfast. Before the day ends, I'll walk, work, shop, drive, cook, listen to music, speak, and seek silence.

When we stop and think about it, we have to admit that the mundane is a miracle. It puts us in touch with the "More Than." There is an invisible depth, a wonder of being, a mystery of dying and rising embedded in every created person and action on Earth. We are all an immense intimate secret known only to God.

Most of the time we are not fully alive. We only exist. We are dazed by so much doing that we forget how to be. We lose our sense of gratitude for life's abundance. The air we breathe, the food we eat, the assistance available when we dial 911—all this and much more we take for granted.

We may even overlook the spectacular singularity of the people who love us. Before long we grow indifferent to the plight of the poor. We don't even thank waiters and waitresses for their service. It is as if we walk through life with opaque patches over our eyes.

There are so many ways to live intimately, why do we miss them? By this I mean to see into people, events, and things epiphanically. Poets and mystics catch in the familiar a glimpse, however fleeting, of the unfamiliar. Why don't we?

These ways of seeing greatly enhance our spiritual life. Our powers of attention, appraisal, and appreciation improve noticeably. We are less agitated, more patient; less decentered, more centered; less fatigued, more rested.

Others may glimpse in our facial features a visible diminishment of stress. The space around us may become more welcoming. Even relative strangers may find us warmer and more outgoing, less analytical and judgmental. We balance hard work with sufficient recreation. Our experience of worship takes a turn for the better, too. We begin to celebrate the sacredness Jesus saw when he blessed and broke the bread (cf. Luke 24:30).

## PRACTICING RIGHT RHYTHMS OF NEARNESS AND DISTANCE

The first way of living everyday intimacy points to the avoidance of extremes. Too much nearness (*invasion of space*) can lead to clinging codependency that smothers initiative. Invasion is a perversion of intimacy. It mistakes feelings of fusion for mature love.

Too much distance (*evasion of space*) leads to the opposite—a kind of narcissistic independence that couldn't care less about people's pain. Evasion is another obstacle to intimacy. It is characteristic of a society where people are unkind, curt, discourteous, and impatient.

Balance is not easy to attain, yet the recovery of intimacy demands it. The right rhythm entails treating people with dignity, neither invading their privacy nor evading their pleas for help.

To avoid invasion, step back when the situation demands it, take distance, regain perspective. Don't try to control people to the point where they might betray their call. Respect their limits as well as their gifts.

To avoid evasion, smile, show genuine concern. Don't cut a conversation short when someone needs to talk. Be especially attentive if you tend to sidetrack or deny the real issue.

Another example might show how this rhythm works in everyday life. Imagine you are in the produce department of a supermarket. Pocket your shopping list for a moment and allow yourself to look in awe at the gorgeous array of fruits, vegetables, plants, and flowers clustered in colorful rows. Appreciate the astounding abundance of goods to nourish us and pleasure the pallet. Sense not only your need to shop but your nearness to nature. Now distance yourself from the immediacy of this scene and place it in the wider perspective of the farming community, the truck drivers who transported what you and others can now buy, the fine meals shoppers like you are planning once they return home.

Even a simple exercise like this one that takes into account the rhythms of nearness and distance enables us to see ordinary life in an extraordinary light. By balancing times of nearness to people, events, and things with conscious efforts to step back and behold their beauty from a distance, we draw closer to the mystery of intimacy that both embraces and transcends everything.

The next time you host a gathering of family and friends, without anyone noticing what you are doing, move away from your guests for a brief duration, out of the range of hearing, and take in glance by glance each person's face and figure. This look of love is another example of ordinary intimacy. Feel empathy for their stories, for the sad and glad memories even a gesture can evoke. Seeing in slow motion or seeing from a distance thus makes our return to normal nearness even more meaningful.

Daily intimacy is an opportunity we often miss because we are too busy or too preoccupied with self to be present to the richness unraveling at our feet. What a loss it is when our agendas break the gentle, energizing rhythm of stepping aside to see the transcendent truth concealed from tense, timebound eyes.

Don't be discouraged. It is possible to restore the balance. Spiritual formation follows the rhythmic beat of distance and nearness. It calls for respect for each person's uniqueness. This is an essential condition for the possibility of seeing not only our individuality but also our commonality in community.

## Balance Solitude and Solidarity

Intimacy without solitary attunement to the Mystery is a virtual impossibility. By the same token, solitude without intimacy may become no more than an exercise in empty self-centeredness or equally empty seduction.

Whether we are single or married, we need intimacy with God to fill our solitude and intimacy with others to assure our solidarity in respectful togetherness. In other words, aloneness before God is as important as oneness with all those entrusted to our care.

The solitude of which I speak ought not to connote remote deserts peopled only with heroic ascetics. All of us need to find quiet times and places to renew our fidelity to God and to express our gratitude for every intimate encounter we have with the ordinary: the taste of freshly baked bread, the touch of a child's finger on our cheek, the sound of a beautiful symphony. . . . There is no end to the reminders of the unique and common ways in which the Mystery invites us to intimacy.

*Solitude is God's way of announcing the silent splendor of the everyday, the shared treasure of the ordinary.*

The more we stand alone with the Alone, the more likely we are to encounter others in their sacred originality. To enter the space of our solitude is to find ourselves in a mysterious way in solidarity with all seekers. According to Adrian van Kaam: "Spiritual life is trustworthy to the degree that it is faithful to the everydayness of the common life, lived as the manifestation of a deeper mystery, by a person who keeps in touch with all of its ordinariness and inconspicuous routines."[2]

As we come home to ourselves, we begin to feel at home with others. By listening to the silence within, we can better hear the voices beseeching us from without. Thus our uniqueness becomes a pointer to universal needs. Our seeming separateness reveals what we have in common. Our solitude is the flip side of our solidarity. Our aloneness signals oneness in the Lord.

## FOLLOW THE EBB AND FLOW OF GIVING AND RECEIVING

Another way of living everyday intimacy is to experience life in general as an ebb and flow between giving of ourselves (our advice, talents, prayers) and receiving from others (food, employment, friendship).

Growth in the life of the spirit is inconceivable without the disposition of donation or self-giving. Whether we receive little or no acknowledgment for our good deeds or so much credit it embarrasses us, we cannot stop giving. Whatever the circumstances in which we find ourselves, we cannot withhold the gift of ourselves. By the same token, if we do not receive encouragement and support from others, we will not be able to keep pouring ourselves out for them. As intimates know, receiving is as important as giving.

A teacher will say that while imparting knowledge to a class, she or he also receives the gift of the pupils' curiosity and enthusiasm for learning. A missionary sister I know gives until it hurts, feeding the hungry and tending the sick, while insisting that she receives from the poor more than she can possibly donate of her time and talent. Still, she appreciates my asking her what she, as a caregiver, is doing to nourish her own soul.

Donation without reception is a formula for failure of social and spiritual presence. It is difficult to remain sensitive to the intimate needs of others—their voiced and unvoiced concerns—if we act as if we have no needs of our own.

By making sure that the ebb of giving (effusion) is balanced by the inflow of receiving (infusion) we are not likely to lose either our patience or our peace. St. Bernard of Clairvaux aptly pointed out the process when he said: "First be filled, and then control the outpouring. The charity that is benign and prudent does not flow outwards until it abound within."[3]

Bernard uses apt imagery to specify his point. He says that in church and society there are more people who act like canals than reservoirs. Canals simultaneously pour out what they receive; reservoirs retain the water until they are filled and then discharge the overflow without loss to themselves. Canals are many, he says. Reservoirs are few:

> So urgent is the charity of those through whom
> the streams of heavenly doctrine flow to us, that
> they want to pour it forth before they have been
> filled; they are more ready to speak than to lis-
> ten, impatient to teach what they have not
> grasped, and full of presumption to govern others
> while they know not how to govern themselves.[4]

There is no place in the arena of recovered intimacy for
false pride or boasting. All that we have, we have been
given. We must do what we can to address legitimate
needs without trying to "play God."

Goodness received and given in this way offers us
many chances for personal and spiritual enrichment.
When a caregiver, such as that missionary friend of mine,
admits that she is in need of care, she is more likely to
invite intimate sharing and trusting solicitude. Giving
care enables us in noticed and unnoticed ways to express
our love for others and our fidelity to the Lord. He himself tells us that what we do for the least of our brothers
and sisters we do for him (cf. Matt. 25:45).

Receiving care reminds us that life itself is a gift to
treasure and that intimacy is its finest gem. It comes to us
freely in all its bright beauty. It is given to us without
price. We cannot schedule its delivery. All we can do is
stand in readiness to receive it.

Who of us can alter by one centimeter the course of the
sun's rising and setting? Yet when was the last time we let go
of our schedules and beheld in silent wonder this daily miracle as a sign of divine intimacy, a revelation of God's unfail-
ing care? We may be capable of measuring the sun's output
of energy, but do we take time to behold its beauty?

Our epiphanic response to cosmos and creation as
pure gifts has to be cultivated if we hope to enjoy everyday

intimacy. The more we live in love, the more people, events and things disclose their hidden radiance and announce a deeper meaning. When we learn to see into life as it is, our homecoming to intimacy will be complete.

Whether we are hermits or homemakers, merchants or mendicants, poor or privileged, we shall be people on the way to holiness and harmony. Our illusions of perfection melt like ice shavings on hot asphalt, only to be replaced by the sweet taste of real life in its fragile yet intimate unfolding. We see everyone and everything in a new light, proclaiming with the psalmist, "O Lord, I love the house in which you dwell, the tenting-place of your glory" (Ps. 26:8).

1. See, for example, Evelyn Underhill, *Practical Mysticism* (New York: E. P. Dutton & Co., 1943), 11–12.
2. See Adrian van Kaam, *In Search of Spiritual Identity* (Denville, N.J.: Dimension Books, 1975), 192.
3. See Sermon 18 in *Bernard of Clairvaux: Sermons on the Song of Songs*, trans. Killian Walsh, Cistercian Fathers Series: No. 4 (Kalamazoo, Mich.: Cistercian Publications, 1971), 136.
4. Ibid., 134.

Lord of earth and sea and sky,
Teach me to live in this world
Without asking why,
To attend to the wonder of being,
To the mystery of dying and rising.
Grant me the wisdom
To see life epiphanically,
To rest my tense, timebound eyes
On the bright beauty,
The divine harmony,
Of your community.
Help me to draw closer
To the mystery of intimacy,
Embracing and transcending
Everything.

# ❦ 4 ❧
# The Many Splendors of Ordinary Intimacy

CHRISTIAN FAITH ESSENTIALLY CONSISTS IN AN
ABILITY TO SEE WHAT GOD CHOOSES TO SHOW
AND WHICH CANNOT BE SEEN WITHOUT FAITH.

—Hans Urs von Balthasar

Ironically, we often appreciate some things only when they are missing from our lives. For example, at our table when I was growing up we always had a bottle of my maternal grandfather's homemade red wine. If we wanted a little taste we could have it. When he died, that traditional winemaking died with him. It's a taste I crave of late but cannot satisfy. I never realized until now how good it was.

When I hear the phrase, "taste and see the goodness of the Lord," a similar wave of nostalgia overtakes me. I return in memory to times of first innocence when that tasting was a regular occurrence. Like many recipients of grace, I did not realize or relish the sweetness of the gift until my only food, to say the least, was ashes.

If there is one pleasure we miss in today's world, it is the simple joy of trusting one another. Women in crime-ridden neighborhoods routinely arm themselves in fear of attack. Rape is no longer a rarity. Moreover, parents warn children—and rightly so—never to talk to strangers; teachers refrain from touching youngsters lest their gestures be interpreted as seductive; the young worry about their survival as natural disasters proliferate around the globe; and the old complain about being left alone or being victimized by con-artists. As a neighbor said to me, "Nothing is sacred anymore."

In such a climate, to speak of the many splendors of everyday intimacy seems almost ludicrous. Yet it is a conviction we cannot disclaim. In the writings of spiritual masters, and in the normal lives of people whose names never make the headlines, incidences of intimacy with God and others are recorded as gifts. We remember, we celebrate, and we believe in the ordinary ways of togetherness that keep trust and hope alive.

Instead of moving away from or against one another, we begin moving with and toward our brothers and sisters as "ministers of a new covenant" (2 Cor. 3:6), as heralds of the "good news" of our oneness with the Triune God.

## THE SPLENDOR OF SHARING

Our God is intimately relational. Jesus so loved the world that "he emptied himself and took the form of a slave" (Phil. 2:7), becoming like us in all things but sin. He laid down his life for his friends. We must go and do the same (cf. John 15:13). He wants us to experience not only the joys of intimacy with the Trinity but the simple pleasures of shared care and concern.

Once for a transatlantic flight I had pre-ordered a vegetarian meal. I knew from previous travels that lighter eating would help me overcome jet lag. When mealtime came and the stewardess had no record of the order, I felt disappointed. Since food was not my major priority, I said to her in a friendly tone, "It's no big deal. I'll eat what I can from the regular tray." So I munched on a side salad with some cheese and crackers and thanked her for her concern. Around me I overheard several people complaining about one thing or another in haughty, unfriendly voices. Each time the flight attendant served beverages I made it a point to smile and say, "Thank you," nothing special, only normal politeness. The next thing I knew, she passed by and whispered, "I have a treat for you." A few minutes later she returned with a steaming plate of asparagus, baby corn, buttered carrots and boiled potatoes, all from the first-class cabin. "I really like to do things for friendly flyers like you," she said. "The complainers are a different story!" Neither of us knew one another. The chances of our meeting again are slim. We never even exchanged names. Yet we enjoyed a splendid moment of ordinary intimacy at high altitude somewhere over the Atlantic.

Simple sharing in our current violent era seems almost heroic. It does not take much effort to smile. A frown actually consumes more energy, and unlike a smile, it is not stress-resistant.[1] Check your body posture. Is it welcoming or stand-offish? While not wishing yourself on people who want to be left alone, do you at least try to make them feel at home? How are your conversational skills? Are you flexible or do you have a one-track mind? Do you show interest in people who come your way? Are you too busy or suspicious to be appreciative?

36

*The way we share or do not share with others affects the way we go toward or withdraw from God. Prayer means to share.*

St. Teresa of Avila believed that the best prayer was intimate conversation with the God who loves us. No technique produced better results than those we see in her life. Because God was Teresa's familiar, he led her to depths of union few attain. She learned, through encounters with Jesus, to love with a great freedom of spirit, to share everything with a generous heart.

## THE SPLENDOR OF GENEROSITY

A child is brushed off because "Mommy is busy." People of different races and religions look suspiciously at one another. Lonely faces of the elderly and infirm appear at the window as neighbors walk by. Will they wave? Sons and daughters cannot find a minute to call. So many occasions missed for ordinary intimacy! Buying more toys, taking a business associate to lunch once in a blue moon, visiting a neighbor in the hospital may be nice, but it is not enough. Lacking in these cases is the spontaneous generosity lasting intimacy allows.

Bound as we are in the West to clock time, we neglect to give one another quality time. That is where intimacy thrives. That is when it takes root. Going an extra mile, not being deterred by unscheduled needs for nearness, thinking of others before ourselves—all are sure signs of a generous heart.

A sturdy bridge to recovered intimacy is the commitment to care selflessly for those whom God sends our way. If we are generous to them, giving of our energy, talents, and time, more often than not they will return the favor. The risk is there that we may be taken for granted. No one ever said that the recovery of intimacy would be easy.

## THE SPLENDOR OF COMPASSION

Doesn't it amaze you that human beings can be hurt a hundred times over and still manage to bounce back? We crush and kill one another, often in the name of social or religious beliefs, yet life goes on, even in war zones. Harsh words as well as deadly attacks batter the vulnerable shores of body, mind, will, and spirit. So overwhelming is the suffering in this world that one could weep a river.

That is why, whenever we show compassion for our own or others' vulnerability we are soothed with the splendor of intimacy. This gift is given and received every time a parent tucks a tired, tearful child in bed or a caregiver does something to soften the pain. In this spirit-to-spirit exchange, expressed as tender mercy, intimacy is born and compassion flourishes.

Our hearts ache for the innocent who are stripped of life and dignity in senseless conflicts. We feel their pain in our living rooms, so vivid is the portrayal of that pain almost nightly by the media. Far from ravaged lands we light candles of compassion. There is no room for complacency. Even suffering felt through empathy transforms us. None of us can control the mapping of our destiny. We acknowledge the shared intimacy of our utter dependency on God.

## THE SPLENDOR OF NOT BEING JUDGMENTAL

The tentacles of prejudice based on race, religion, or sex run deep in the human condition. How many opportunities to experience everyday intimacy have passed us by because "We don't associate with their kind"? There are times in our life when practical judgments have to be made. A certain person may not be suited for this or that task. What hinders the quest for intimacy in daily life is not a person's skills or lack thereof, but secret turnoffs rooted in prejudice.

Worst of all is the penchant to judge anyone with ultimate certitude. Motivating this intractable stance is not lack of affinity or religious differences. It is as if our conviction of another's moral debilitation is a response to a pronouncement from on high! Exactly who do we think we are? Playing God is one sure way to kill the process of intimacy's recovery.

Instead, own up to your prejudices. Assess their source. Decide to change. Hold firm to your desire to seek the truth. Then you will be part of the solution not the problem. You will clear away many obstacles to intimacy. An enemy may become a friend—miracles do happen! Racism and sexism must diminish. Why not spearhead this needed renewal now?

## THE SPLENDOR OF BENEDICTION

It's taken me many years to recognize that I was denied a source of ordinary intimacy due to a wrong philosophy of life. I am referring to the directive that said, in so many words, "Withhold praise to preserve a person's humility." Like sensitive children everywhere, I would have welcomed a spoken or unspoken blessing from adults near and dear to me. For "all the right reasons" (which turned out to be wrong) I did not receive it—mind you, not out of malice or meanness but because people honestly underestimated how poor our self-images might be. What they thought would prevent the build-up of pride only served to weaken an already fragile sense of worth.

Is it any wonder that pop psychology counsels us to "hug someone" or to look in the mirror and say "I love you" to ourselves? The lesson I have learned the hard way has to do with bestowing benediction as another key to ordinary intimacy. It means literally to speak (*dicere*) well (*bene*) of or to another.[2]

Blessings from the heart are always transforming. The legend of *Beauty and the Beast* is a classic example. Only when Belle finds it in her heart to offer the Beast her blessing does he begin to change. In the tale the metamorphosis from grotesque deformity to princely perfection only happens when Belle kisses the beast. She has already detected a heart of gold in a figure horribly deformed; this final gesture of intimacy works like magic.

Our blessings may not yield such dramatic results, but we may be surprised at the difference a compliment makes. "Your cooking is out of this world," says a newlywed to his wife, and she sparkles with pleasure. There is a fine line between offering benediction and exaggerating. No set rules govern this kind of intimacy. My own feeling is that it is better to err on the side of "too much" than "not enough." Basic directives must not be violated. For example, a child blossoms when we wipe put-down words from our vocabulary.

I have never found a person unattractive who is able to praise. Such people exude benediction. It is as if they feel intimate toward everyone and everything. There is nothing affected about them. Their gift of beatitude is genuine. People glow in their presence with a feeling of importance, and they see themselves as special treasures. It then becomes second nature for them to repay the compliment.

Our world needs people who bless every passing yet precious moment of life. They are like epiphanic messengers from the Father of Light, from whom comes every worthwhile gift and every genuine benefit (cf. James 1:17).

1. See Susan Muto and Adrian van Kaam, *Stress and the Search for Happiness* (Williston Park, N.Y.: Resurrection Press, 1993); Susan Muto and Adrian van Kaam, *Harnessing Stress* (Williston Park, N.Y.: Resurrection Press, 1994); and Susan Muto and Adrian van Kaam, *Healthy and Holy under Stress* (Williston Park, N.Y.: Resurrection Press, 1994).
2. See Susan Muto, *Blessings That Make Us Be* (New York: Crossroad, 1982).

Lord of love and light
From whom flows every blessing bright,
Teach me to imitate your caring,
Sharing generosity.
Draw me into splendid
Moments of recovered intimacy
Full of compassion and tender mercy.
Teach me to be trusting
Of my own and others' vulnerability.
Make me a recipient
Of your graces,
Bestowed abundantly.

# ✿ 5 ✿

# Becoming an Epiphany of Everyday Intimacy

WHAT A THRILL TO ADD TO THE PRAYERS OF THE
SAINTS THROUGHOUT THE AGES OUR "OWN LITTLE
TWITTER."

—C. S. Lewis

The word *epiphany*, from the Greek *epiphaneia*, means, according to *Webster's New Collegiate Dictionary*, appearance or significant manifestation. It suggests that each of us is to become a witness to the mystery of God's presence and light in this world. In us others ought to see a sign of divine mercy, peace, gentleness, and joy.

When Jesus said to his followers that to see him was to see the Father (cf. John 14:9), he was being an epiphany of the Most High. He brought to light something of the ongoing, interforming, radiating love of the Father for the Son through the Holy Spirit. So intense was Jesus' life of intimacy that when he withdrew to

Mount Tabor to pray he was transfigured before his apostles' eyes. He was illuminated with epiphanic radiance (cf. Luke 9:29).

As persons baptized in the name of the Triune God, our goal is to become "little words" within the Divine Word. We are to be models of trinitarian faith, hope, and love. Everyday existence ought to be a living example of an intimacy with God and others that will last for time and eternity.

Is it possible to reach such a lofty goal and still remain down-to-earth? What is our point of entry to this way of epiphanic living?

## SEEING SIMPLY

"Living the life of the spirit is simple," an old monk said to me. "What makes it complex is sin." I've never forgotten these words. What is simple is whole, uncomplicated, lacking in guile. I wish I were able to see everyday things in their simplest terms as pointers to the Transcendent. That seems to be the reason for monastic life as well as a basic tenet of our faith: to see beneath the surface meaning of life to its hidden depth. Eyes of faith cut through the dense underbrush of doubt to the clear vision of truth.

I know that when my faith is strong, I can see in every limit a new possibility. The main focus of my attention has to be Jesus for this kind of seeing to occur. In his light, I begin to see myself, and all people, events, and things in a new way.

Like a seasoned merchant, I trade the complexity of sinful willfulness for the simplicity of a Christ-filled life. I let go of my agendas. I try to see his face, to follow his call. In the mirror of mercy, I behold myself as I am. False pride deflates; defenses drop. Without shame I beseech the heavens for help.

Seeing simply is painful. Nothing can be hidden from an honest gaze. Either our lives are an epiphany of God's presence or they are not. Some of what we see in the mirror may have to change. The standard for transformation is not our seeing a direction and taking it, but our seeing God's guiding hand and being thus led.

Seeing what's out-of-sync in our life could be discouraging were we to engage in self-scrutiny only. That is why we must turn to Jesus. Our efforts to attain instant perfection are futile. Rather, we must try gently to flow with the pace of improvement set by grace.

Seeing simply keeps our final goal—intimacy with the indwelling Trinity—in focus. When we see everyday life against the horizon of its final end, simple objects like a fishing pole or a favorite mug suddenly take on epiphanic meaning. One glance evokes a galaxy of recollection of what was, a rush of anticipation of what might yet be.

Surface seeing recedes as our eyes open to the truth that all is gift, ourselves included. Worldly clutter keeps the complex in view. Simplicity reveals the whole and Holy. Rediscovering the simple calls for an intimate eye trained to catch the radiance around us redolent of our benevolent God.

## LISTENING ATTENTIVELY

Epiphanic listening also has the power to transform hearts. As our inner ears become attuned to the Word of God, we begin to hear the "music of eternity."[1]

Such listening frees us from distractions. It enables us to enjoy every revelation of ordinary intimacy. The aim of such listening is not to analyze the logic of every disclosure but to enter into what the Spirit seems to be saying to us.

What sets our rational minds in a spin often makes sense to our hearts, provided we listen with love and let go of the fear of losing control. Are we willing to "come and see" (cf. John 1:39), or do we demand precise answers?

Inner stillness places us in a posture of readiness to receive invitations to intimacy. We have to refrain from jumping to conclusions. The Transcendent speaks in the immanent in ways that may surprise us.

It is tempting to listen for dramatic clues to the divine will instead of attending to our here-and-now situation. That is the most likely place where God communicates needed guidance.[2] Our present circumstances convey hidden messages if we learn to listen, first of all, to God's holy Word.

Attentive listening benefits us in another way as well. At low points in our lives, when words are useless, a kind of wordless exchange unites our spirit to God's. Silence, the deepest form of listening, draws us to new depths of intimacy at such moments. We want to do only what the Lord asks of us, be it action or endurance.

Our whole life ought to become an exercise in listening attentively—to the words of Holy Scripture, to the writings of the spiritual masters, to the wise counsels of good people, invested with authority.

Despite our zeal for the Lord, we must be patient. The way will not be revealed at once; the process of growing in ordinary intimacy takes a lifetime. As a musician seasons his or her style, years may go by before we develop an ear to appraise rightly every epiphany of the Mystery. We may even mistake God's voice for our own, but at least we are trying to listen.

To a hearing heart, a message once garbled becomes clear; a path thought to be lost is found. At times, though rarely, genuine locutions may accompany faith-filled listening. The back-and-forth discourse between us and the Divine is like the ebb and flow of the sea. We do not wait for thunderous disclosures. We listen to the still, small voice at the core of our being and try our best to respond. Once we allow the Spirit to take the lead, useless worry recedes. We learn the wisdom of surrender.

## DWELLING REPEATEDLY

Of the many avenues to ordinary intimacy none is more to be trusted than dwelling repeatedly on the basic texts and themes of Christian spirituality. Simplicity, obedience, self-emptying in humility, these are only a few essentials that call for repeated reflection.

The words of Scripture and the masters are like home-ports after stormy explorations on unknown seas. The repetition of timeless truths, appearing and reappearing in the Bible and the literature of spirituality, becomes a point of reference amidst the push and pull of daily life.

> *Intimacy does not require us to be innovative,*
> *but to be faithful.*

Reiteration of the common ways of faith deepening is not a matter of blind conformity but a way to appropriate timeless truths. These cannot be absorbed in one reading or on one occasion of listening.

47

Because the word of God is "alive and active" (Heb. 4:12–13), it invites us to new discovery each time we encounter its power. We cannot predict where the Mystery will lead us. For every answer we receive, another question arises. No sooner is one need met than another presents itself.

God's silence is as intriguing as God's speaking. Silence ought not to be understood as a sign of rejection. Neither should it be for us a source of frustration. It is an invitation to return again to what it is that draws us inward. The full meaning of a religious experience may only be understood years after its initial occurrence.

For example, consider how long it took St. Augustine to understand his conversion experience in the garden or St. John of the Cross to grasp the meaning of his imprisonment in Toledo. New levels of meaning emerged for both saints because of their repeated dwelling on these watershed experiences.[3]

The same is true in our own life. Every time we return to an epiphanic revelation, the door of insight opens a little more. Quiet rumination calms our concerns. We cease strenuous attempts to master the Mystery and start to appreciate the intricate tapestry woven by grace.

Despite the ups and downs of daily living, we feel blessed repeatedly. Every obstacle becomes a formation opportunity, an opening that releases, not an end point that blocks, our inner potential. Seeing how others have met the challenge of their call encourages us to affirm our own. We then stand firm in our commitment to recover the art of living in everyday intimacy. We discover that Jesus is with us in the valleys and on the heights, that he is as much at home in a machine shop as in a monastery.

Repeated dwelling draws us into a heart-to-heart relationship with the Lord. It is both prayerful and playful, tranquil and intense, contemplative and active. Our lives are less likely to meander from point to point. It evidences both freedom and direction, and no bars bind the human spirit. It soars like a solitary bird to meet the Holy Spirit. It gathers strength for the journey because it stops repeatedly to seek proper food.[4]

## Waiting Patiently

We ready ourselves for a life of everyday intimacy also by learning to wait patiently. As I recall Adrian van Kaam saying, we cannot push against the pace of grace. Otherwise we lose our peace. We clog the channels of seeing simply, listening attentively, and dwelling repeatedly already opened to us.

The joy of living in everyday intimacy is enhanced when we wait upon divine disclosures like watchmen for the dawn. We let go of the "shoulds" and "oughts," the "musts" and "nevers," of rigid control and learn to flow with grace. We allow ourselves the luxury of resting in the Lord's embrace. We keep vigil even when it seems as if God has lost our address!

We cannot carry our crosses alone. If we wait patiently, the Lord will come to our rescue. He endured more pain than we will ever know. How can we let our spirits wilt in the dry winds of discouragement when mercy rains down upon us in such torrents?

Such waiting is not a matter of will power. It is a release of longing love. It does not ask for absolute certitude. It wants only to respond courageously to the call.

Patient waiting requires that we let go of self-centered plans and projects. It asks us to remain open to a level of intimacy beyond our control. Relax your anxious striving for solutions to every problem. Many of life's mysteries remain impenetrable. Occasionally insights from on high surpass any self-initiated solution.

Waiting invites us to stay wakeful and alert to every epiphanic disclosure of divine-human intimacy. We must not be pushy. Help will come if we humbly ask for it. God does listen. The response given may not follow our script but in the long run God's way is the best way for us. Our task is to trust, not to demand instant clarity, to wait patiently, not to be pushy.

To wait is not a passive act. It is an active receiving of and responding to the will of God. The wait will be challenging, inviting, and appealing. We are to wait *upon* the splendor of the ordinary rather than waiting *for* the extraordinary. In due course we shall come to understand, as Job did, that divine wisdom transcends anything we can hope to grasp. We repent of idle expectations in the face of God's all-powerful Word (cf. Job 42:1–6).

As we wait with reverence, we no longer worry about what may happen to us. The past is behind us, the present is now, the future is in God's hands. Great mysteries are unfolding at our feet. Thanks be to God, we now have the eyes to see them.

❦

1. See Adrian van Kaam, *The Music of Eternity: Everyday Sounds of Fidelity* (Notre Dame, Ind.: Ave Maria, 1990).
2. See Susan Muto and Adrian van Kaam, *Divine Guidance: Seeking to Find and Follow the Will of God* (Ann Arbor, Mich.: Servant Publications, 1994).

3. See St. Augustine, *The Confessions of St. Augustine*, trans. John Ryan (Garden City, N.Y.: Doubleday & Co., 1960); and John of the Cross, *The Collected Works*, trans. Kieran Kavanaugh and Otilio Rodriguez (Washington, D.C.: Institute of Carmelite Studies, 1991).
4. See Susan Muto, *John of the Cross for Today: The Ascent* (Notre Dame, Ind.: Ave Maria Press, 1991); and Susan Muto, *John of the Cross for Today: The Dark Night* (Notre Dame, Ind.: Ave Maria Press, 1994).

Epiphany of the Most High,
Transfigured, radiant,
As the bright sky.
Make me a witness
To your mystery.
Help me to see simply,
To listen attentively
To the pace of grace
You've set for me.
Indwelling Trinity,
Ready my heart to receive
Invitations to intimacy.
Let me dwell repeatedly,
With no illusion of mastery,
On the unknown seas,
The intricate tapestries,
Revealing and concealing
Your providential destiny.
Let me wait patiently,
In a posture of receptivity,
Upon every formation opportunity
Your loving will unwraps for me.

## ❦ 6 ❧

# Appraising Our Progress in Becoming Intimate People

GOD HAS FIRST HAD TO DO A WORK *IN* YOU, SO
THAT [GOD] MAY OCCASIONALLY DO OR SAY
ANYTHING *THROUGH* YOU.

—Francis of Assisi

Deepening our intimacy with ourselves, others, and God is a never-ending process. It takes a lifetime to become appreciative instead of deprecative, generous not stingy, open-hearted, not mean-spirited. Ask yourself if your life is softening around the edges. Toward the suffering do you feel more tender? Toward the cruel righteously incensed? Has your heart leapt up in awe as you watch waves crashing against a windswept shore? Did you ever see the Mystery manifesting itself in nature as on a fresh spring morn? When a child is born? In a tedious task as in the smell of freshly washed laundry swaying in the sun? Have you felt the power of pure faith in the folded hands of an old peasant at prayer?

When it comes to appraising our progress in becoming intimate with people, how do we know if we are on the right path?

## "YES" TO HOLY PROVIDENCE

The events that mark our journey from birth to death bring with them joy and sorrow, laughter and tears.

Everyone reading this sentence can testify to its truth. Doesn't it seem like yesterday that you were a child? Were you sad or happy? Did you feel understood by your parents or were you trapped in a straight-jacket of disrespectful demands and expectations?

A memory can sustain us or pain us. People we love can help us or hurt us, but they also give us a choice: to grow cynical or to become more Christ-centered.

The life of the Risen Lord could be summarized in one word: *yes*. There is a significance to human suffering when we make the sign of the cross. Take the case of parents who, with the best of intentions, did not nurture their child's life call. They wanted to remake him or her in their image, not in the image of God in whose likeness all are created. They may have been master mood-breakers, never stopping to ask what he meant or what she was feeling. The parents acted as if they were omniscient. The child felt powerless.

Later in life we have to make a choice. Will we live in reaction formation, becoming more defiant or foolishly choosing a deviant path to "show them"? Will we consign our parents to God's mercy and heal any hurt or bad memory by forgiveness? All of us are lovable in God's eyes. God finds us infinitely worthwhile, despite our sinfulness. No matter what happens Someone up there has our best interests at heart.

Such a faith-filled outlook is not a cop-out but a survival measure. What is the alternative? To see only brokenness and no beauty. Be like a good teacher. She has an uncanny ability to catch the creative potential in persons others say are hopeless.

With a heartfelt "yes" to Holy Providence, we become celebrants of ordinary intimacy. It is a gift no one should be without.

## PRESENT TO GOD'S PRESENCE IN OURSELVES AND OTHERS

When eyeing a suspicious stranger or dealing with an abusive or addictive parent, it may be difficult, if not impossible, to see the inner light. Hearts tend to close up like clam shells in such cases. It is easier to blame than to pardon, to accuse than to console. Yet in each human being there is a divine spark that unites them, despite sin, substantially to God. It takes an intimate eye to see that we are all God's children, created with a dignity and destiny nothing but our own stubborn resistance and refusal can destroy.

Every time we doubt redemption or listen to the lie that we can solve our problems without the help of God, we open ourselves to demonic seduction. We move away from, rather than into, the arms of our Redeemer. We block the saving grace of holy intimacy.

Such mindfulness does not mean that we condone evil out of a false sense of tolerance. It does mean remembering in whose presence and by whose power we have come into being. Inhumane actions do not decrease the abyss of divine mercy. We are to pray for those who persecute us and even, within reason, to place their needs before our own. We must try to catch a glimpse of the divine likeness mirrored in our own lives as well as the lives of others.

## TREATING SELF AND OTHERS AS IMAGES OF GOD

Whether our needs are material or spiritual or both, we sense the difference between people who treat us harshly—as if we were specimens of meat subject to inspection—and those who truly want to help us as we are. It is one thing to write a check to finance a shelter for unwed mothers and another to meet them and their children face-to-face. Both treatments may be legitimate for different types of givers, but too many seem to prefer to keep their charity at a distance.

In a dehumanized society, the Golden Rule can be seen as a formula for ordinary intimacy. Treat others as you would have them treat you. This is a divine directive that has to be taken off the back burner if we want to build up bonds of respect.

When I meet you on common ground as the brother or sister you are, your race, color, creed, or country of origin, takes second place to your being a child of God. How could I then do anything but treat you decently?

## LIVING THE SACRAMENT OF THE PRESENT MOMENT

Growth in trust, attention, and respect creates around us a circle of intimacy. We slow down the pace of life's progress. It becomes easier to detect the thin red line of God's guidance.

We begin to hear the beat of a different drummer. Grace is leading us to a new way of beholding reality. Like conoisseurs we return repeatedly to the craftwork of the Master Artist. We understand the saying attributed to Teresa of Avila that the wheels of God grind slowly but they grind exceedingly fine. As apprentices of intimacy, we do not want to miss the details of the drawing or the new meanings we see.

A friend of mine told me that she likes to drive slowly on a country road that has become for her like the entrance to a secret garden. She lets each tree reveal its spectacular singularity, each crooked fence and fertile field its story. Similarly, when she sets the table for guests, she stops at each place to say a prayer for the person soon to dine there. She is one of the friendliest people I know, a keen observer of the human condition and a compassionate caregiver.

If we fail to see the present moment as a sacrament, we may forfeit the best chance we have to leave an imprint on those we love. It's as if we prefer the darkness of a burrow to the beauty of the full light of day.

The gift of recovered intimacy lets us unwrap life layer by layer as we would a precious package full of surprises. We enjoy the infinite richness of the ordinary not just during an occasional retreat from the din of daily demands but all the time.

We are still and still moving. Life becomes more like a rhythmic dance than a rubber band stretching us toward momentary contemplation and snapping us back into action with no rest in between.

Intimates of the Mystery avoid compartmentalized living: here is my worship, here is my work. They enjoy the rhythm of the dance. Life becomes a graceful flow from presence to participation, from stillness to speaking, when we celebrate the sacrament of everydayness.

## SEEING THE WORLD AS THE HOUSE OF GOD

Having built my own home in 1985, I know from experience what a sense of happiness, what a step toward security, home ownership offers. Still, in contemplative pauses I realize that in the long run I'm living on borrowed time in a rental property I'll never really own—not even when I make my final mortgage payment!

These homes of ours rest on the good earth that belongs to God. In this mansion there are many chambers (cf. John 14:2), but each of them has to be entered through the "narrow door" (Luke 13:24). As we grow in intimacy with the ordinary, we learn God's house is not a possession we can buy or sell at will.

Picture yourself on an interplanetary flight. From the porthole of your spaceship, you see the world as the house of God. Awe fills your whole being as you behold from afar the life-sustaining planet you call home. You perceive it as a place of goodness, beauty, and light. It is a fragile ball we free-willed creatures can abuse or befriend, treasure or trample.

The intimacy of an encounter with the Mystery may become so intense that we see not only the present moment as a gift of grace but the entire cosmos as transfigured by the Risen Lord. Such a vision transcends particularity while taking every detail into account. We behold the whole as holy. All of the universe and its history, from the beginning to the end of time, becomes for believers a radiant epiphany of the Risen and Glorified Lord.

The greeting of the Orthodox Church not only at Easter time but throughout the year is, "My Joy! Christ is Risen!" People profess in this simple phrase the truth that sin and death have lost their hold on our hearts thanks to the redeeming intimacy that exists between us and the Second Person of the Blessed Trinity. Never alone, we adopted sons and daughters share in the eternal community of interforming trinitarian love.

As our vision widens through the power of contemplative prayer, we begin to see the world and everything in it, ourselves included, in a new way. This freshness of seeing is a sure sign that we are moving from apprenticeship to proficiency in intimacy.

## GIVING THANKS ALWAYS TO GOD FOR A MULTITUDE OF GIFTS

Each step on the journey to joy in the everyday draws us to pray. Our heartfelt "yes" to Holy Providence is a prayer. So is our growth in trust and the respectful treatment of others. Our pledge to treasure everything from the tiniest sign of divine goodness to the entire earth is a prayer of thanksgiving.

Whether we know it or not, we have begun to pray always (cf. 1 Thess. 5:17 and Eph. 5:20). We not only reserve prayer for special occasions; we become living prayer—people who, in the words of the Eastern Church Father, St. Gregory of Nazianzus, "remember God more often than we breathe."

To pray unceasingly is to sense that our thirst for God is as great as God's thirst for us. Such prayer is a stirring in the depths of our hearts for an intimate person-to-Person relationship with the Father in Jesus through the Spirit. Nothing less than the restoration of our likeness to God, disfigured as it is by sin, can satisfy our hearts.

It is impossible to separate how we pray from the dispositions of praise and appreciation. The force of intimacy may rise to such a level of intensity that were it possible we would pray all day long: "Praise God from whom all blessings flow, praise him all creatures here below, praise him above ye heavenly hosts, praise Father, Son, and Holy Ghost."

To pray without ceasing is to thank God for promises fulfilled and hopes for what the future holds. It is to see spreading before us hot deserts, fertile valleys, deep forests, and rolling hills. There are miles to go before we reach the place of grace God has prepared for us from eternity. Hand in hand with our intimate companion, we can advance with a lighter step. With a smile on our face and a song in our heart we approach heaven's door, knowing all the while that Jesus is carrying us there on a wing and a prayer.

Artist of intimacy,
Accept me, an apprentice,
Seeking proficiency.
Fill me with fidelity
That I may see
In brokenness, rare beauty
In everydayness, an invitation
To say yes.
Second Person of the Trinity,
Make me a celebrant
Of ordinary intimacy,
Able to see in the destitute
Divine dignity.
Let me treat with decency
What is fragile and spare.
Increase my capacity
For unceasing prayer.
Draw me, a child of God,
Beyond particularity
To the splendid vision
Of a cosmos transfigured
By your redemptive decision.

# ❦ 7 ❦

# Practicing Ordinary Intimacy

To choose what is difficult
all one's days
as if it were easy,
that is faith.

—W. H. Auden

Intimacy, like friendship, is not something we can force. It comes to us as a gift. Once we *attain* this grace, the question arises: How can we *retain* it? What must we do not to deviate from the right road or take unnecessary detours? Under what circumstances must we protect this gift as if it were a precious heirloom?

## LOVE THE SMALL AND THE BEAUTIFUL

Imagine a rosebud, moist with morning dew. See it glistening in the early light. Behold its fragile yet perfect formation. Smell its sweet fragrance. Pretend you are filming its blooming in slow motion. Petal upon petal unfolds, fresh and beautiful to behold, bud blossoming into a lustrous red rose.

Intimacy enables us to see great beauty in the small things of life. It guards us against losing the spark that makes life worth living. It reminds us of God's omnipresence in and around us. Like the imperceptible but steady upward press of spring flowers through the last remnants of snow, like the almost unnoticed growth of children, cultivating ordinary intimacy is a quiet, undulating process, a blessed rhythm of seeing and not seeing, of revealing and concealing.

Our body ages, our mind expands, our spirit strains toward the light of truth. Less and less escapes our appreciative look. We take as much delight in the rising sun as in a child's first step or a friend's warm embrace.

In our kitchen or in the car, at church or in an office meeting, we try to stay in tune with the Lord's leading. We love life's little gifts as much as he did:

> Therefore I tell you, do not worry about your life, what you will eat [or drink], or about your body, what you will wear. Is not life more than food and the body more than clothing? Look at the birds in the sky; they do not sow or reap, they gather nothing into barns, yet your heavenly Father feeds them. Are not you more important than they? Can any of you by worrying add a single moment to your life-span? Why are you anxious about clothes? Learn from the way the wild flowers grow. They do not work or spin. But I tell you that not even Solomon in all his splendor was clothed like one of them. (Matt. 6:25–29)

Learning to see every moment of life as a small miracle moves us quickly to new depths of insight and intimacy.

## Take up Your Cross as the Key to Renewed Intimacy

Jesus' invitation to carry the cross does not compel us to take on extraordinary feats of physical, emotional, or spiritual suffering. It is often enough to listen to our body, to its litany of aches and pains, to its constant reminders of mortality.

We suffer when we have to bear the cross of an impolite person, who slams the door in our face; of a domineering spouse or parent, who never listens; of any number of traumatic experiences or annoying aches and limits. Take that pesty neighbor who walks in the door without knocking and expects the coffee to be hot. No wonder we bristle. It is an effort to make pleasant conversation when we want to be left alone. We do not have to look elsewhere for the cross.

Heeding the call to discipleship is not meant to be coercive. It implies a free, relatively unfrustrated, response. What we say or do depends in great measure on the quality of our nearness to Jesus, our reliance on his mercy. If we are his intimates, we will always pray: "Lord, show me what you would do in this situation."

The cross of everydayness becomes a key to intimacy on one condition: that we let go of grandiose expectations and accept what is. You may have wanted another set of parents or your parents a different lot of children, but these are the people God has placed in your life for a reason. It takes a while to see why. Hence the cross is at once a mystery of love and a challenge to change.

The cross reminds us that we always approach the Lord with empty, outstretched hands and so we pray: "Fill them, Lord, with whatever graces I need to pursue your holy love-will. My timetable and yours may differ, but so be it. You know what is best for me." It is not our place as God's intimates to rewrite the script but to rise to the challenge of the play as it is written.

The clarity of vision Christ gives us when we take up our cross can be startling. What we saw as failure, he seems to find effective. When we imitate Christ and abandon ourselves to the Mystery, then no secret God wants to show us is likely to be missed. The more we pray in the spirit of Jesus, the more of himself he will reveal to us. Thus is our growth in intimacy nourished by his mercy. Only in this light do we begin to see that suffering has a meaning.

## SEE SUFFERING AS A LINK IN THE CHAIN OF WISDOM

At first the message of suffering may be obscured. It is as if we are trying to decipher a garbled code. Then one day the puzzle breaks open. We are blessed with an "Aha!" moment.

Now we understand what God was trying to show us through the tortured reasoning, the nights of weeping, and the spiritual dryness we have had to endure. The paradox of the cross becomes more transparent. What looked like the end of the line turns out to be an incredible learning experience. Dying is a passageway to rising. Misery is an opening to mercy. Seeming abandonment by God does mark the start of trustful abandonment to God.

At this turning point from death to life, we totter on the brink of a second conversion experience. We

approach the time of second innocence. We cannot
return to the naiveté of childhood, but we can recover
the wonder of pure trust. Suddenly we feel energized,
courageous, creative. People may comment on how joyful
we look, on how peaceful we are. "How can you be so
happy after all you've been through?" We know the
secret, though words fail to communicate what we feel.

We smile, mumble a few inadequate explanations,
thank the person for the compliment—but who could
verbalize the intimate bond, the warm embrace, of Jesus.

The man Job had such an experience. After useless
attempts to explain why he had been brought so low, he
was led to a vision of God's eternal plan in its awesome
perfection. His convoluted questions, his immature complaints, exploded into splinters. In a flash of comprehen-
sion he admitted:

> I know that you can do all things.
>> and that no purpose of yours can
>> be hindered.
> I have dealt with great things that I do
>> not understand;
> Things too wonderful for me, which
>> I cannot know.
> I had heard of you by word of mouth,
>> but now my eye has seen you.
> Therefore I disown what I have said,
>> and repent in dust and ashes.
>> (Job 42:2–6)

At this sacred moment of felt intimacy Job found his
place in the order of creation. Kneeling before God in
adoring surrender, he became a man of wisdom, a messenger of grace.

Like Job, we too can go from agony to ecstasy over a lifetime or in a single day. One minute we feel overwhelmed by the burdens we must bear; the next we feel carried beyond these problems. The fruits of prayer defy explanation. In due course—often when we least expect it—we see what the Mystery had in mind. We vow from now on to let God take the lead. Control has only gotten us in trouble!

The pathway to wisdom is not easy to traverse. The clarity we come to through grace is worth the effort. If God grants us such an "Aha!" moment, to outsiders our life may seem the same but we sense a difference. To have been touched by the finger of God, if only for a brief duration, is to know a truth no argument to the contrary can refute.

Any epiphany of the Divine draws us to a depth of intimacy hitherto unknown. Something of what we were may be gone forever. Who we are to be has been found. Our immediate needs may or may not have been gratified, but that is no longer important. What matters is not instant satiety but an increase in fidelity.

## DON'T LOSE THE KEY TO FREEDOM OF SPIRIT

Saints and spiritual masters from early ages to the present day assure us that the graced experience of *knowing* God intimately—as distinct from merely *knowing about* God intellectually—takes a tremendous weight from our shoulders. We are freed interiorly by grace from narrow intellectualism blinded by conceit. Now we see!

Such inner liberation has nothing to do with escapism. Life with its crosses and blessings, its dilemmas and delights, continues to shake us loose from the moorings of complacency. The difference is that we have the freedom to be true followers. We are not attached in an ultimate way to anything or anyone who is less than God. We know, in the words of St. Teresa of Avila, that God alone suffices. All we want is to give and receive love in the spirit of Jesus.

Liberty of spirit leads to intimacy. It attracts to itself, like magnets draw metal, an abundance of reverence and respect, affirmation and appreciation, humor and humility.

As much as people who live in recovered intimacy may want to escape notice, they often stand out. Their caring presence imprints itself on our memory. They seem more able than the rest of us to shake off the weight of useless worry. Their overall demeanor manifests a graciousness anyone would like to emulate.

God's intimates live with life's inevitable limits without complaining. At the same time, they are ready and willing to alter any course of action that detracts from the freedom meant for them by their Lord. To paraphrase a familiar prayer, they accept with serenity what cannot be changed, they find the courage to change what they can, and they ask for the wisdom to know the difference.

## Maintain a Faith Perspective

The liberated person is inwardly free because he or she is intimately bound to God, not seeking to escape the crosses of life but asking to see whatever happens from a faith perspective.

From this vantage point, life is no longer a struggle for power, a goal to be possessed, or a series of isolated pleasures. Everyone and everything finds its place in the time allotted to us by the Eternal.

Uplifted by graced moments of intimate encounter, we are less tempted to abandon our commitments when the road gets rough. We accept disappointment as a normal consequence of daily living. Sorrow does not cause major setbacks. We take the peaks of life as much in stride as the valleys.

Seeing with the eyes of intimacy enables us to recognize the truth that we are at once a community of sinners in need of forgiveness and a community of saints, who, by the grace of God, are swimming in a sea of compassion. A wonderful story from the Jewish tradition illustrates this point:

> Three angels were called before God and sent down to earth with orders for each to locate and return with the most precious thing in all the world.
>
> The first angel found himself in a prominent yeshiva (school) and brought back to God a sample of that earnest and dedicated yeshiva air. God seemed impressed, but said nothing.
>
> The second angel descended and found herself in the midst of a joyful synagogue service. The angel snatched up one of the most heartfelt prayers of the congregation and presented it at the throne of God. Again, God seemed impressed but uttered no words.
>
> The third angel came upon a busy street. Masses of people were crowding the sidewalk, hurriedly trying to go about their own way. Cars and cabs and busses were clogging the streets, honking their horns. Everyone seemed to be in his or her

own world, oblivious to the other people around them. The angel saw that no one seemed to notice the man in rags lying on the sidewalk; everyone just walked around him. Everyone, that is, except for a single teenage boy.

The angel watched transfixed as he went over to the lonely man in the crowd. He had no money to give him, but he had time and he had the desire to provide some much needed warmth and friendship. He and the man sat together for a few minutes, and it was obvious that the lad's kindness made a real difference to the lonely, ragged man. This was clear to the angel too, for he noticed a single tear in the corner of the man's eye. It was a tear of joy and gratitude, and it was about to roll down his cheek. The angel snatched the tear up and, before it could reach the man's cheek, hurried back to Heaven, and appeared before God. He held the tear up for God to touch; it was still warm.

The angel looked to God for some sort of reaction. God did not speak. The Creator could not speak. Instead the angel saw a tear, but not the one he had brought back with him from earth—no, this tear was welling up in the eye of God. It was this tear that told the angel he really found an example of human compassion, the most precious thing in all the world.

Epiphany of the Divine,
Omnipresent Lord of all,
Lead me to renewed fidelity
Amidst reminders of mortality.
I need the gift of intimacy
To behold in each dying, a rising,
In each cross, the sign of God's guiding.
Clarify my vision so I may see
In small things transcendent mystery
Revealing the meaning of suffering,
The movement from agony to ecstasy.
What I seek is not satiety but liberty.
Make me inwardly free
Because bound to Thee.

# ❧ 8 ❧

# The Blessings of Intimacy

SANCTIFICATION CONSISTS OF ENDURING MOMENT
BY MOMENT ALL THE TRIALS AND TRIBULATIONS IT
BRINGS, AS THOUGH THEY WERE CLOUDS
BEHIND WHICH GOD LAY CONCEALED.

—Jean Pierre de Caussade

A recent viewing of *The Wizard of Oz*, a film I've loved since childhood, led me to ponder anew the blessings of ordinary intimacy. When Dorothy felt forlorn and full of doubts (Did the legendary Emerald City really exist?), she followed the Yellow Brick Road expecting a revelation. She soon made friends with the Scarecrow, whose fear of failure rivaled her own feelings of homesickness. Alone, they were like aliens in a hostile land. Bound together in friendship, they felt as if they could conquer any obstacle, including the Wicked Witch of the West! Nothing could deter their dreams if they had each other.

The same sense of restored confidence affected another character she befriended—the rusty Tin Man. He became as supple as a squeaky hinge that has been newly oiled when he absorbed the balm of Dorothy's love. She gave him a heart. The intimate secrets of the journey she would now share with her new friends gave the third character she met, the Cowardly Lion, a reason to live.

Replacing fear with trust, convincing ourselves or someone we love to make a new start, turning cowardice to courage: all are the results of taking the risk to live in recovered intimacy.

Dorothy knew by the end of the story that the real treasure to be found in Oz was not the granting of her wishes but the lasting gain of loving and loyal relationships. Her character radiated common sense, care, and courage. In this classic tale, intimacy made the strange familiar, the exotic commonplace, the invincible vincible. Even the Wizard turned out to be one of us, an ordinary person in need of a place called home.

This film is a classic because it calls to mind our need for overcoming fear, for seeing bright rainbows behind every cloud. It reminds us believers of the lessons of love taught by the Lord. He wants the virtues of compassion and gentle concern to shine through us. We do not have to be wizards. We do not need to rely on magic tricks or cleverly constructed contraptions. We only have to be ourselves. The give-and-take of intimacy comes naturally if we open our hearts to others as Dorothy did.

## PRACTICING THE POWER OF PRESENCE

A teacher to whom I'll always be indebted was an inspiration to our whole senior class. Her love for English literature was apparent in her way with words and her guidance of our compositions. What inspired us was not so much what she said but the way she was. Her presence was at once intimate and discrete. She had the right balance of nearness and distance, gifts any educator would envy. She taught from the heart. She related to each of us in a personal way, yet never overpowered us with her personality.

I believe we encountered Christ in her. She loved us and listened to us. She moved us from where we were to where she knew we could go with the right kind of encouragement. I now know what I could only guess then—she respected our uniqueness. She called us by name. Somehow she was able to shape and form an unruly conglomerate of "know-it-alls" into a learning community.

I think this was possible because my teacher saw the presence of Christ in us. She had a knack for what I would now tag "epiphanic intimacy." The effect of being with her made a lasting impact. Who she was still reverberates in me and hence her presence lives on.

For Brother Lawrence of the Resurrection, a classic Christian spiritual writer who spent most of his life in the kitchen of a Carmelite monastery, the practice of the presence of God did not come easy at the outset. He advises us that in the long run it produces "imperceptibly wonderful works in the soul." This practice "draws down from the Lord an abundance of grace and leads insensibly to that simple gaze of love, to that sight of God's continual presence, which is the most simple and the most fruitful kind of prayer."[1]

We need to see the fruits of epiphanic intimacy in Christians like Brother Lawrence and my beloved teacher. They help us to live the Gospel not only in church but in the world where we labor and enjoy leisure, where we engage in everyday work and play. We need to emulate such people if we want to preach the Gospel in word and deed, if we want to give silent witness to its truth in a world hungering for wisdom.

## OFFERING A WARM WELCOME ALONG THE WAY

A first blessing of recovered intimacy is the feeling of belonging or being welcome. A person like my teacher offered those who came to school—commuters and neighborhood kids alike—the atmosphere we most needed to love learning. We were not only informed by her; we were formed in fidelity to our life call. I associate with her what I believe to be among the most intimate words Jesus ever spoke: "Come to me" (Matt. 11:28).

In this invitation we hear a message of profound consolation. When we are weary, we can rest in the arms of Jesus. We can hold his hand when we find life too much to bear, when everything, ourselves included, seems about to break. We can always count on Jesus to refresh us. At any moment we can turn to him. If we are thirsty, he will give us a drink. If we are hungry, he will set a banquet table. There is no charge for such intimacy. As the prophet Isaiah says: "Come, without paying and without cost, drink wine and milk!" (Isa. 55:1).

Intimacy freely given and freely received is a true gift. We can go to the Lord without having to wait for an appointment. He listens when we need to talk. He befriends us when we feel lonely. He shows us how to live in faithfulness when we are tempted to go astray. We do not have to solve our problems alone. The Lord is at our side. He is a welcome partner in our daily round.

To respond to the Lord's gracious invitation, we must be willing to bring our whole life before him, to hide nothing. I learned from the first to the eighth grade in my Catholic elementary school to "talk to Jesus."

In the warm welcome of a faith community, we never feel alone. Others show us every time they hold out a helping hand that it is good to share whatever is on our minds or in our hearts. The welcome mat is always out for us. All we have to do, once we step across the threshold, is to knock on the door. The greeting of love we expect to receive is guaranteed.

## A LASTING COVENANT

We do not have to put on airs. We can be as open about our burdens as a child confessing his or her faults to an understanding parent. We may feel ashamed about the bad things we did, but we have no doubt about the outcome. Offered to us is the cooling refreshment of forgiveness.

Jesus gives us food for the journey on days when we feel weary as well as when our energy abounds. All that matters is that we come to him in trust, for, as Isaiah says, the Almighty will "renew with [us] the everlasting covenant" (Isa. 55:3).

The covenant is the intimate bond between us and God. It will never be broken as long as we lay our burdens at the feet of Jesus. Held in his outstretched arms, we find the consolation and strength we need to continue on the way.

## FOSTERING THE FLEXIBILITY OF FAITH

Responsive intimacy grants us another blessing: the gift of formative flexibility. What kills this response is deformative rigidity. People fixed in their ways leave no room for welcome, no time to establish deeper bonds.

To flow flexibly with the guiding wisdom of God is a challenge grace helps us to meet. We live like explorers familiar with the terrain yet open to surprises. We see ourselves as companions of Christ and as intrepid explorers who can always return to their Father's house. We ask for direction. We resist the temptation to take self-righteous detours. We know that the way things have always been done may not be the way of the Lord.

Armed like knights of faith with composure and flexibility, it is not likely that the jousts of life will be able to dampen our resolve. Like Mary's, our souls magnify the Lord (cf. Luke 1:46–47). We want to be good servants able to cope with the pressures of a busy world while keeping in mind the master whom we serve.

Rigid rules governing relationships paralyze intimacy. They kill the spontaneity that moved Jesus to cast the money-changers out of the Temple (cf. Matt. 21:12) and to forgive the woman caught in adultery (cf. John 8:3–11). Jesus broke political and societal taboos so as not to compromise the truth.

We live in a culture guided not by the gentle invitation of Jesus but by functional pragmatism (does it work?) and monetary rewards (how much will we make?). Countless buyers and sellers promise us material prosperity but often at the price of spiritual impoverishment. The psalmist foretells what happens then:

> But my people heard not my voice,
>      and Israel obeyed me not;
> So I gave them up to the hardness of their hearts;
>      they walked according to their own counsels.
>
>                                (Ps. 81:12–13)

Consider your own life. Does rigidity disconnect you from the whispered intimacies God wants to communicate to your soul? Does willfulness block your ability to listen with flexibility to the graced directives God gives you at every moment? The Holy Spirit not only speaks in our hearts but in the prosaic events that make up our day.

## CELEBRATING EVERYDAYNESS

Everydayness is like a swirling sea. There is always furniture to dust, housework to do, appointments to keep, meals to prepare. In the endless round we may find little cause for celebration. The broken shells, the bits of seaweed, the scattered debris of daily life cannot be overlooked. It would be nice to find a cleaner beach, but this is where we are. What is, is. Reality is the "stuff" of spirituality. We drift, to be sure, into the illusion of devising our own version of the will of God. Were it up to us, it would lack ambiguity, pain, and frustration, but it would not be real.

After all, Jesus walked the dusty roads of Nazareth. He worked in a carpenter's shop. Mary and Joseph had to run a household. They had to make ends meet. Neither for them nor for us was God's will a rigid preconceived blueprint forecasting worldly perfection. Life as it is with its myriad imperfections is the place of grace, the arena of our salvation.

> *Intimacy with Christ invites us to listen to life,*
> *neither overreacting nor growing indifferent.*

In *The Wizard of Oz*, Dorothy does not try to remake her three odd friends. She accepts them as they are with their fretful, frenetic, fearful characters. Her love for them never wavers. As a result she gives them a new lease on life.

When we share with others the gift of intimacy grace has granted to us, several blessings fill the air around us and create a formative atmosphere:

1. We grow in the conviction that God has a special purpose for our life. He cares for us intimately, watches over us always, and provides for us abundantly.

2. We sense a oneness with Christ that reveals itself in our life and work. Our presence may prompt others, without our knowing how, to reconsider the integrity of their own call.

3. We are as open to the challenge to change as we are to reclaiming the richness of what is.

4. We value every person, young or old, God entrusts to our care.

5. As our prayer life grows more intimate, we feel less alone. We thank God that we belong to a faith community.

6. When life becomes burdensome, we let the Lord take our yoke upon his shoulders (cf. Matt 11:30). We silence our disquiet and learn to flow with grace.

7. We try to interweave our abiding with the Lord in quiet contemplation with our willingness to help others in need. Social justice, peace, and action are the fruits of contemplation.

Step by step we follow our own yellow brick road to the high places of prayer and presence where Christ awaits us. We may not be wearing magic slippers, but we are responsive to every movement of the Spirit. We celebrate everyday work and play, dancing in time to the music of eternity.

1. Brother Lawrence of the Resurrection, *The Practice of the Presence of God*, trans. Donald Attwater (Springfield, Ill.: Templegate, 1974), 123–24.

Y ou who said, "Come to me,"
From whom I can hide nothing,
Reveal the secrets of the journey
To epiphanic intimacy,
To the give-and-take
Of everyday work and play.
Replace deformative rigidity
With formative flexibility,
Not killing spontaneity
But helping me to dance
In time to the music of eternity.
Give my life a new thrust
Moving me from fear to trust,
Encouraging a fresh start,
Transforming the heart
In such a way
That no longer does it go astray.
Grace sets the pace,
I rest in your embrace.

# ❦ 9 ❦

# Witnessing to Recovered Intimacy

CONTEMPLATION IS NOTHING BUT A SECRET, PEACEFUL,
AND LOVING INFUSION OF GOD WHICH, IF ADMITTED,
WILL SET THE SOUL ON FIRE WITH THE SPIRIT OF LOVE.

—John of the Cross

The perennial principle that "like attracts like," the old saying, "Smile and the world smiles with you," the proverb that we can attract more people "with honey than with vinegar" are all true in my experience. People respond positively when you offer them a friendly hand, do a favor, or compliment their accomplishments.

An African student of mine felt homesick because the city was such a cold place, and not only in winter. Icy frost can invade the human heart, too. "How could it be," he said, "that people from the same community hardly have the courtesy to give one another the time of day?" He left shaking his head in disbelief, but his remark came to mind the next day when I was in the supermarket.

Before a holiday everyone feels frantic. I saw any number of people forgetting to say a simple "Thank you" at the checkout counter. That's when I made a split-second decision with long-range repercussions.

Now I pause at a busy intersection to see if anyone needs help crossing. When the traffic light switches from red to green, and someone has to change lanes, I wave the other driver on. If I know a friend has had a bad day, I pick up the phone to call when I think he or she is at home.

Such gestures and acts exemplify everyday intimacy. Without them, the quality of life goes rapidly downhill. More of us need to commit ourselves to cultivating this gift in our hearts, in our homes, and in society as a whole.

## SHOW SOME APPRECIATION

Everyone likes to receive a word of thanks, yet too often we withhold it. Most people—parents and children, shopkeepers and mechanics, teachers and medical doctors—merit appreciation. We have to undo the poor formation that told us to hide our feelings.

I remember being warned that if I was too nice to people they would take advantage of me. Praise could give you a swelled head. It was wrong to treat a person special because others would be jealous. Thus I lost many chances to show appreciation when it was both due and needed.

All of us seek to love and be loved in return. That is why the goal to recover intimacy is so important. Think of Jesus in this regard. He saved the wedding party at Cana from embarrassment by following his mother's request and making sure the guests had enough wine (cf. John 2:1–11). He allowed a woman to break social rank and to anoint his feet with expensive perfume (cf. John 12:1–8). He showed

83

affection and appreciaton for people like Simon Peter's mother-in-law, whom he healed from a high fever (cf. Thess. 4:38–39) and the widow whose son he raised from the dead (cf. Luke 7:11–15). He allowed others to express their appreciation for him as did Mary, who sat at his feet and listened to him (cf. Luke 10:38–42) and the little children whom he allowed to touch him (cf. Luke 18:15–17).

Imagine how many chances we've lost in the space of one lifetime to imitate this intimate kind of Christian interchange. How often have we been too busy to listen, too bound by rules of "right behavior" to respond spontaneously to another's need?

When a child wants to tell her mother something and she says, "Later," a potential moment of intimacy between them disappears forever. When an AIDS patient needs a hug and his caregiver draws back out of fear of touching him, both people are diminished. Another invitation to transcendent intimacy falls into oblivion. Missed is the opportunity to go beyond what divides us, to celebrate the common humanity we share.

In the end failure to show some appreciation hurts us more than it does other people. Imagine the intimacy depleting case of a married couple who cannot communicate their feelings to one another. Forced words and stressful silences build up between them like icicles that melt one day and freeze solid the next. All it may take is one sign of mutual appreciation to make them feel as if the meltdown of summer has come early.

## GIVE OF YOURSELF

Self-giving is another fruit of restored intimacy. People produce more in a user friendly atmosphere of mutual give-and-take than when they are treated like parts of a machine, easily replaced by newer models.

In community and in the marketplace little real growth will be recorded unless we learn to give of ourselves. Selfishness is like an infectious disease. It is silent but deadly. It kills us individually and as a society.

When the boss thinks only of himself, the whole company deteriorates. Morale drops. Petty crime increases. An "I'll do my duty but no more" mentality prevails. When parents put their own needs first on the list, more children have to be put in foster homes. Still more are at risk for their life due to abortion or abuse. Intimacy goes far beyond temporary infatuation. It moves us toward commitment. It asks us to give not only of our time and talent but also of our heart.

By contrast, misguided adolescent passions center on "me"—on *my* pleasure, *my* feelings, *my* needs. That's all that matters. Narcissistic sentiments have about as much staying power as water beads on a hot griddle. They vaporize at the first sign of hardship. They are as ephemeral as sex without love.

Without an intimate sense of self-donation, people are at risk to demean one another. Lovers become expendable like cheap objects to use and discard. Ignoring the call to be with and for others becomes all too common. How often have you said, "I don't want to become involved"? Where lack of intimacy leads to abuse, cruelty knows no bounds.

We Christians must take a stand. Listen to Jesus. He says we will be known by the love we show for one another (cf. John 3:16–18). He gave of himself to such a degree that he was willing to lay down his life for us (cf.

John 15:9–15). Are we willing to do the same for our friends? For what we believe?

Neither you nor I are capable of this kind of caring, courageous intimacy unless we ask the Lord for help. The downward pull of self-aggrandizement conflicts with the upward push of grace. Only if we accept the Lord's self-gift to us can we become a gift to others. Then there is a chance that fidelity will replace infidelity, trust cast out distrust, devotion purify dependency, sensibility soften sensuality. Gradually, remnants of childish narcissism give way to the mature rewards of recovered intimacy. We choose the way of Christ over worldly gains.

The need to overpower others gives way to the desire to empower them to use their gifts. Pleasure as the sole focus of a relationship now asks what is pleasing to God. Possessions are no longer clung to as guaranteed sources of happiness but as goods to be shared.

Everyday intimacy is the parent of profound transformation. It puts our vital energy, our emotions and motivations, to good use in service of God and others. Not only do we sense ourselves making progress spiritually; we also feel better physically. Others notice that we are happier, more relaxed and easygoing. "What's your secret?" they ask. How can we explain that the giving of ourselves has made for such gain.

Try to follow the way of intimacy. You will soon feel less split, more whole, less torn between your feelings of loneliness and your fear of involvement. You'll be more open to finding and keeping new friends and helping others. Thanks to your efforts, what I call "Just Noticeable Improvements" (JNIs), start to happen.

A minister gathers homeless kids on a bus and brings them to a church-sponsored school. A mechanic takes his time to repair an airplane because he feels personally responsible for its passengers. A mother no longer denies her drinking problem but seeks proper care for her family's sake. Where charity and love prevail, there God is ever found (cf. 1 Cor. 13:13). Unknown and known are the holy ones of God.

## ENTERING THE COMMUNION OF SAINTS

St. Clare of Assisi (c. 1193–1254), like St. Francis, her mentor and guide, chose as her mission to work and pray for the salvation of souls. From the start Clare was countercultural by virtue of her cloistered vocation. She was also wise and prudent, avoiding any extremes of mortification that might have called more attention to her than to the Lord. She asked only for the courage to follow her call to love her sisters, the church, and the world as Jesus did in obedience to her rule of life.

By choosing the lifestyle of enclosure, Clare learned paradoxically what it meant to love inclusively. By possessing nothing, by embracing holy poverty, she, like Francis, could belong entirely to God. Together they would devote themselves to the service of others.

In one of her letters to Blessed Agnes of Bruges, her friend and the foundress of several monasteries, Clare expounds on the meaning of life:

> Our labor here is brief, but the reward is eternal. Do not be disturbed by the clamor of the world, which passes like a shadow. Do not let the false delights of a deceptive world deceive you. Close your ears to the whisperings of hell and bravely

oppose its onslaughts. Gladly endure whatever
goes against you and do not let good fortune lift
you up: for these things destroy faith, while these
others demand it. Offer faithfully what you have
vowed to God and [God] shall reward you.[1]

Clare, great intimate of God that she was, loved the world,
but she was not duped by its worldliness. Neither did she
believe in false humility. She insisted that we take justifi-
able pride in our accomplishments and in the competence
God has given us. We need to celebrate our gifts and serve
others if we expect to be witnesses to everyday intimacy.

In another letter she wrote to Blessed Agnes of
Prague, she offers her formula for discipleship:

> With swift pace, light step,
> [and] unswerving feet,
> so that even your steps stir up no dust.
> go forward
> securely, joyfully, and swiftly,
> on the path of prudent happiness,
> believing nothing,
> agreeing with nothing
> which could dissuade you from this resolution
> or which *would place a stumbling block* for you
> on the way,
> so that you may offer *your vows to the Most High*
> in the pursuit of that perfection
> to which the Spirit of the Lord has called you.[2]

Clare counsels us to be honest about our limits as
well as to express gratitude to God for our gifts. What
matters is that we remain true to ourselves and to our
Beloved. As we walk the road to intimacy, we have to be
prepared to replace our initial romantic ideals of what it
means to follow Christ with the hard reality of the cross.

Despite the martyrdom we may have to undergo, we will find the same treasures God gave to his witnesses, Francis and Clare: inner peace and radiant joy.

More often than not there are no answers to our questions, humanly speaking. Then with Jesus we feel, "My God, My God, why have you abandoned me?" But grace also gives us the courage to say with Jesus, "Into your hands, I commend my spirit" (Luke 23:46).

What Clare tells her sisters, we can take to heart. Let us place our whole lives under the bright radiance of God's glory. No amount of abuse, no degree of violence or ugliness, can despoil the intimacy in which we are held by our beloved from the beginning.

If Clare can witness to such a vision, then so can we. For, as she writes to Blessed Agnes of Prague: "I beg you in the Lord to praise the Lord by your very life, to offer to the Lord your *reasonable service* (Rom. 12:1) and your *sacrifice* always *seasoned with salt* (Lev. 2:13)".[3]

It would be impossible to find a better window to ordinary intimacy than the one Clare opens for us. Pray for the grace to offer praise. Serve God with joy. Season with the salt of love every sacrifice God asks you to make. Then you will be a witness to everyday intimacy as a way to holiness both humanly lived and divinely inspired.

1. *Francis and Clare: The Complete Works*, trans. Regis Armstrong and Ignatius Brady, Classics of Western Spirituality (New York: Paulist, 1982), 207.
2. Ibid., 196.
3. Ibid., 202.

Lord, you never missed
A chance to show kindness,
To follow your mother's request,
To think only of the guests.
You exemplified ordinary intimacy
As an epiphany of your mystery.
I need to learn from you
Simple lessons, ever new:
To smile, not to frown,
To sense when friends feel down and alone
To pick up the phone,
To appreciate, never to denigrate,
To grow in transcendent intimacy.
I want to love others inclusively,
To shun shows of false humility,
To embrace the cross
Whatever the cost in self-loss.
Let me choose the way of Christ
Over worldly gain,
Trusting that joy arises
Out of deepest pain.

# ❧ 10 ❧

# Intimacy, Spirituality, and Sexuality

THIS IS THE IRRATIONAL SEASON
WHEN LOVE BLOOMS BRIGHT AND WILD.
HAD MARY BEEN FILLED WITH REASON
THERE'D HAVE BEEN NO ROOM FOR THE CHILD.

—Madeleine L'Engle

Human sexuality is interwoven with the entire fabric of our emotional, intellectual, and spiritual life. My being female is integrated with and inseparable from all that I am and do. My outlook on experience, my feelings, attitudes, inclinations, and interests, my ability to think, write, speak, teach, and administer—all are filtered through the fine mesh of femininity.

I believe that the bridge between sexuality and spirituality is ordinary intimacy. Its trusses weaken when the media portray sex as a source of pleasure separable from responsible unitive and procreative love. Christians feel a formidable challenge in this regard.

How do we, as single or married persons, commit ourselves to Gospel values in a world ensnared in careerism, consumerism, materialism, hedonism, and secular humanism? How do spouses remain faithful to Christ's way of loving when the media portray casual affairs as the rule rather than the exception? Though recent polls show that most people remain in monogamous, faithful relationships, the culture pushes the contrary, assuming that infidelity prevails.

Longing for love yet not finding it pushes many singles to seek a mate at any cost. Here, too, social pulsations press one toward the deceptively easy route of self-gratification. The fulfilling ideals of Christian discipleship and celibacy often fall on deaf ears. Unwanted pregnancy, desertion, and the risk of abortion place cruel crosses on the backs of women who fall for the lie that "love is free."

Compounding the problems of promise-breaking and lack of a support community is the mobile state of employed and unemployed people today. Layoffs uproot families like doomed forests. Relationships suffer. Neighborhoods collapse. People are too exhausted by violence, drugs, and every form of dignity depletion to fight back. Easy escapes in drink or sex drag families to their knees. The homeless, both young and old, prowl the streets.

Connections to one's family of origin, to say nothing of one's extended family, are chipped off like dead branches from a vine. Due to circumstances either beyond one's control or because things are out of control, what suffers most, unless a substitute family of faith can be found, is ordinary intimacy. It is the best protector of committed marital and single sexuality and spirituality.

Christ wants to be with us whether we are destitute because of a lack of life's goods or in ego-desperation because none of them has brought us real happiness. Believers like us need to experience blessed intimacy with the Trinity. This deep undercurrent of love for God overflows into love for one another. Such tender mercy is our best protection against uncommitted sex.

Blessed intimacy is the safest and strongest bridge between our belief in God and our lived obedience to the moral imperatives regulating sexual behavior. To love someone as Christ would demands this kind of fidelity. It provides the link in a golden chain of believers adultery and promiscuity try to break.

In an I-Thou relationship, we commit ourselves to uphold the other's dignity. Blessed intimacy depends neither on spontaneous affinity nor on a cold sense of duty. It is a choice inspired by grace. One simply chooses to love one's friends and family members with mutual respect and reciprocity in imitation of Christ's generosity.

The perversion of intimacy leads to uncommitted sex and infidelity. The other is no longer a "Thou" but an "It," a "play thing" not a partner with whom one is willing to share a lifetime of dreams and disappointments.

Friendship in the single life and in the married life keeps the Lord at the center of the relationship. He makes room in our hearts for shared hopes and sorrows. Sheer sexual gratification leaves no space for spirit-to-Spirit bonding. One's "god" becomes one's body—adored and adorned as an object of gratification. One behaves as if sex were separate from the wholistic embrace of responsible unitive and procreative love.

Blessed intimacy counters this sad, demeaning scenario. It opens our arms to the invitations, challenges, and appeals that comprise every human relationship. Trinitarian love wants us to become other-oriented, not self-centered. Intimacy reminds us to keep the best interests of our spouse, our friends, children, and coworkers, at the top of our list of concerns. While caring also for ourselves, we try to respond to the voiced and unvoiced needs of others.

Asked of us by intimacy is a wise balance of gentleness and firmness, confirmation and affirmation. We begin to see all people as inhabitants of the house of God, as finite messengers of the infinite, as brothers and sisters in the Lord.

We want to imitate Jesus' capacity to make and keep friendships with women and men. He calls us, as he called the first disciples, to commit our lives to this quest for graced conformity to his way, his truth, his life (cf. John 14:6). Look to Jesus if you want to know how to integrate your sexuality and spirituality through the practice of everyday intimacy.

## TWO WAYS OF LOVING

Both the single and the married life are calls from God. Both require steady Christian formation from adolescence to adult life. Single persons can no more separate their sexuality from their spirituality than married persons can. We humans are fully masculine and fully feminine sexual beings. It is ridiculous, therefore, to reduce the wonder and beauty of our human sexuality to only one area of expressivity, that of genital intimacy.

There are as many ways of showing love as there are people who love. One way happens in marriage with its reciprocal and responsible procreative and familial love. Another way happens in singleness with its reciprocal, responsible acts of love and service.

Sexuality—as distinct from mere genitality—has to remain a sacred component of our single or married state. It is a gift to celebrate, not a source of shame or seduction, manipulation or moral compromise. The key to such quality relationships is charity—the human attempt to love others with the love with which we have been loved by God.

## OBSTACLES HINDERING SEXUAL-SPIRITUAL INTEGRATION

The first obstacle has to do with what openness really means. How much is too much? How little is too little? Erring on the side of undifferentiated openness may tempt us to collect a house full of superficial acquaintances, who never challenge us to seek in-depth spiritual friendships. Erring on the side of isolated withdrawal may mean having no one in our life to hold us accountable for behavior that is out of touch with Christian commitment.

Nowhere is this firm yet gentle response more necessary than in the sexual realm. Out of loneliness a person may expose him or herself to intimate contacts that yield pleasure but do not make one feel precious in the sight of God and other people.

God calls us to be life-givers whether we are biological parents or not. To touch without crushing, to show compassion for another's pain, to know when to hold onto someone and when to let go—these are the hallmarks of the blessed intimacy lived by Christ and to be lived by us.

A second subtle obstacle to sexual-spiritual integration concerns overwork without sufficient recreation. Using the excuse of "omni-availability," calling it a "virtue," may be a defense against the fear we have of relating on a relaxed basis to young and old, to friends and strangers. Because we don't take time to cultivate ordinary intimacy, we risk seeking illegitimate outlets for our intimacy needs.

With the friends we do have, we may experience the third obstacle, that of inordinate exclusivity. While such attachments may make us feel secure, they prevent us from being open to the possibility of widening our circle of relationships. We not only feel envious and jealous of our special friends; we may also forego the chances God sends us to cultivate everyday intimacy with a wider community of people.

This obstacle can breed a clinging kind of dependency replete with dramas portraying betrayed trust or subtle power struggles. Life soon becomes prone to possessiveness.

The problem of total exclusivity in love relationships affects both single and married people. One's circle of companions becomes smaller and smaller. Singles feel excluded from family life; married couples feel bound by it.

Life lived under the shadow of possessiveness signals unfulfillment, not freedom; anxiety, not appreciation; negativity, not nurturing. The right kind of loving in imitation of the intimacy of Jesus has to be at once detached from yet committed to caring for others in the inclusive, freeing way he modeled.

## CONDITIONS FACILITATING SEXUAL-SPIRITUAL INTEGRATION

Fidelity to Christ is only possible if we relinquish our futile attempts to control relationships and operate instead out of a disposition of letting be and letting go. It would be naïve to believe that this wholesome, harmonious style of living can be gained without pain. Life in the world can be lonely, even when one shares a bed. There are times when instant intimacy seems a better choice than trying to turn the sorrow of loneliness into a celebration of solitude.

We are particularly prone to succumb to sexual temptations if our prayer life has become dull, uninspiring, and routine. How different our outlook might be if prayer were an experience of felt intimacy with the Lord! Under the pressure of family or society, we may be pushed into a marriage that is not congenial with our calling, or we may make a premature decision to find a mate.

Listening only to our fears or to the "me only" input of a secular culture can silence the whispers of the Spirit. Thus the struggle to integrate sexuality and spirituality calls for compassion. Especially in a sexually fixated culture like our own, it is an easy slide into the trap of self-centered preoccupation or sexual indulgence.

To reintegrate our sexual-spiritual existence, our relationships must once again be modeled on Christ's capacity for redemptive love. He shows us how to treat others respectfully and, by implication, how to care for natural and cultural things in a spirit of stewardship.

Our equality before God remains the same whether we are male or female, married or single, young or old. All of us must resist and repudiate the sins of sexism, racism, and any other "ism" that separate us from the love we owe to God and to one another

## BECOMING INTIMATE COMPANIONS IN CHRIST

Every time I read the newspaper or watch television, I feel more and more convinced that the world needs the witness of Christlike people whose intimate presence gives us a glimpse of God's boundless mercy. In Jesus' circle of companions, the disciples had different gifts (Peter was outspoken, John was gentle, Matthew was precise, Mary Magdalene was brave), yet all played a role in salvation history.

In the lives of the saints this same unity-in-diversity pattern prevails. It guarantees that membership in the Body of Christ will never be boring. Think of the unique yet communal contributions of Francis and Clare of Assisi, John of the Cross and Teresa of Avila, Francis de Sales and Jane de Chantal, Peter Marin and Dorothy Day, Baron von Hügel and Evelyn Underhill. Their sexual differences were not obstacles standing in the way of witnessing to Christ but gifts to be celebrated for the good of the whole Church.

In the lives of contemplative-active types like Bernard of Clairvaux, Catherine of Siena, Thérèse of Lisieux, and Vincent de Paul, we see another facet of the link between sexuality and spirituality. The passion and power of human sexuality in the mystics becomes a metaphor for the purifying and consuming love of God that prompts them to a life of charity.

With a passionate thrust of pure desire, the saints literally fall in love with God. In their journals, narratives, poems, and essays, holy lovers seek to express holistically the Christ-centered spirituality every one of his friends is called to emulate.

## FRUITS OF BLESSED INTIMACY

One blessing is that we incorporate into our personal rule of life the commitment to try to address the interests and needs of others before our own. Though our intentions may be more pure than our actions, at least we know what we ought to do as spiritual and social persons conformed to Christ. We have a sense of service. We want to share in his transforming mission in a wounded world.

Our hearts are stirred by the pleas for help coming from aging parents, difficult children, lonely friends. However limited our time may be, we are not oblivious to the cries of the needy and the unloved. We try to do what we can for them.

Blessed intimacy can be as barren as a harvested field if we do not remain generative in some way. We die a little if we lose the gift of a warm and tender touch. Love shown in a manner in keeping with our calling invites love returned, the finest fruit of which is spiritual friendship.

Blessed intimacy helps us both to be a friend and to be befriended by others. With colleagues and coworkers, our attitude is such that we value the singularity of every human being. We resist any attempt to level another's originality. We admire everyone's worthwhile accomplishments.

To uphold Christian ideals pertaining to sexuality and spirituality is a lifelong commitment. The alternative is to risk living a split existence where sex is one thing and spirituality another. In the long run, this split is self-destructive. It takes honest self-reflection, prayer, and transformation by grace for healing to happen.

## FIDELITY AND INTIMACY

In any given set of circumstances, there is only so much we can do. We cannot be our own or others' saviors. We have to leave the ultimate integration of our lives to God. Prepare yourself for any number of losses and limits. If you experience a setback, ask God for mercy. Renew your commitment to care for others and yourself as you are cared for by Christ.

Guided by grace, you can live as a sexual-spiritual person, as a vital, effective, inspired and inspiring woman or man, happy to be of service to church and society.

Our mutual dependence on divine mercy makes us more interdependent on one another. Life becomes a song of praise, a hymn of appreciation for the goodness of God and for the grace to stay faithful.

To love in this way requires emotional and spiritual maturity. It calls for a contemplative vision of human beings as members of one family, as children of the same God, who calls each of them by name (cf. Isa. 43:1). To nurture this vision, we must go into the desert with Jesus. Our meeting there in solitude is but the beginning of a lifelong response to loving and serving others in his name.

To affirm the goodness of our sexual-spiritual personhood is a beautiful way to proclaim the bounty of blessed intimacy. In this light the divine imperative to go out to the whole world and proclaim the good news that we are one in the Spirit and one in the Lord (cf. Gal. 1:26) makes perfect sense.

Jesus, I seek as love's purest gift
The bounty of blessed intimacy.
Integrate into my spirituality
The treasure that is my sexuality.
In a world strangled by self-gratification
Let me be a witness to
The grace of self-donation.
Show me how to bestow
Both confirmation and affirmation.
Lead me to the path of reciprocity.
Use the strength of Christian maturity
To untangle the tight web of infidelity.
Break open the traps of hedonism,
Consumerism, and secular humanism
That threaten to override the tide
Of blessed intimacy
Teeming toward our tired shores.
Teach women and men
To love their dignity,
To practice charity
And spiritual generativity.

# ✸ 11 ✸

# Growing in Wisdom, Age, and Grace through Everyday Intimacy

I DON'T KNOW WHAT YOUR DESTINY WILL BE, BUT
ONE THING I DO KNOW: THE ONLY ONES AMONG YOU
WHO WILL BE REALLY HAPPY ARE THOSE WHO HAVE
SOUGHT AND FOUND HOW TO SERVE.

—Albert Schweitzer

I remember how startled I was when a friend of the family who had not seen me for three months expressed amazement about how much taller I had grown since she last saw me. I was a self-aware thirteen-year-old, yet I hadn't noticed the changes that were obvious to her until I looked in the mirror. Physical maturing is a fact of life.

What about emotional maturity? A few years later the same friend found it amazing that I seemed to know what I wanted from life. Granted, I had a lot of growing up to do, but even I sensed something of where my feelings might be leading me. For instance, I knew I wanted to study English and journalism and go to a coed Catholic college.

We know a good deal about physical and emotional maturity, but what about maturation in the life of the spirit? This is not a measurable entity as are the number of inches taller we are or the personality inventory we fit. Neither is spiritual maturity a matter of excessively examining our feelings to determine if we are following our heart's desire or reasoning to the point of exhaustion about our life's direction.

Spiritual maturity is a mystery. To be sure, grace builds on nature. It helps if we receive from God the gift of good parents, solid friendships, supportive peers. Love received increases our capacity to love in return. But grace can also form us into mature Christians through suffering.

What if we have had a bad hand dealt out to us. Maybe our genetic make-up predisposes us to heart disease. Then the older we grow, the more vulnerable we become to stress-related illnesses. What if our parents were too controlling or even abusive? It may take years of counseling, together with the presence in our lives of wise and loving friends who believe in us, to set us on the right path. Yet in the valleys of insecure physical health and scarred emotionality, we may feel the touch of divine mercy and mature in faith.

Of this we can be sure, the practice of everyday intimacy as spiritually mature people depends on the uniquely human capacity to give of ourselves beyond the self-preserving instinct. Jesus declared with certainty: "Love one another. As I have loved you, so you also should love one another" (John 14:34).

To move from vital or emotional to intimate spiritual formation, we must struggle day by day to love unselfishly. Growing in wisdom, age, and grace before God means becoming less resistant to God's call. Obedience is basic to becoming spiritually mature. We are not sufficient unto ourselves. We depend from birth to death on the God in whose image we have been made (cf. Gen. 1:26).

This initial formation as male and female, created according to the likeness of God, is the ground of our original dignity and the source of our spiritual maturity. The opposite, spiritual immaturity, is marked by the fall into conceited self-sufficiency that separated us from our Maker and cast us like exiles into the land of unlikeness. Body, mind, and soul waged war within us. Disobedience reigned supreme. Rather than consign us forever to the bondage of sin, God showed us the depth of his love. In the fullness of time God sent his only begotten Son, Jesus Christ, to be our savior.

The story of our spiritual maturation received a new start. That God loved us first (cf. 1 John 4:10) and would not relinquish us to the evil of sin and death is the beacon of our faith. Such love emulated in the best way we can is the basis for spiritual maturation and ordinary intimacy. Our care and concern for others blossoms because we recognize in them as in ourselves the misery that called forth God's mercy. In an unprecedented way Christ raised our nothingness to nobility.

## OVERCOMING OBSTACLES TO MATURE INTIMACY

For a time when I was growing up, I seemed to be like a rubber band, snapping somewhere between impulsive reaction ("I can't stand her") to reflective response ("I wonder why I'm feeling so miserable or so happy today"). There were times when I wondered—and still do—when anger would give way to acceptance, mistrust to trust, doubt to surrender. I suspect that it will take a lifetime and then some for my love to be purified of self-centered needs. Still these are receding and I can honestly report in journals I keep some JNIs ("Just Noticeable Improvements"), especially where difficult relations are concerned. I am trying to cultivate at home and in the corner of the world entrusted to my care a sense of community with Christ at the center.

Mature intimacy like true love is both generative and realistic. The way I operate alone and with others has to be life-giving and accepting of limits, respectful of privacy while committed to warm encounter.

I do notice that the people I look up to as spiritually mature strive for moderation and balance in all things. In times of obvious desolation or consolation, they maintain equanimity.

Intimacy becomes errant if it is either excessive or indifferent. Some people love too much. They become possessive. Others love too little and retire to their own world.

The problem of possessive love can be treacherous in the close confines of a community or a family. A duplicitous attempt to "own" others may be masked under the guise of "doing everything for their own good." This lie is one that almost always destroys a relationship. It deprives the other of the space he or she needs to grow emotionally and spiritually.

Contests of wills are inevitably exhausting. Employees in a company may feel overwhelmed by dubious

signs of affection bent on having the last word as much as
siblings and spouses do. Such willful competition smothers creativity.

The opposite extreme of aloofness can be as unnerv-
ing. People around us or those dependent on us never
know where we stand. Do we admire or despise them?
They feel like puppets on a string. One moment we show
affection, the next we grow cold.

Such immature ways of loving make us weary. We
need to correct our course—to find the balance—before
breakups occur. Following Christ puts us on the right path.
His way of loving is never manipulative or seductive.
Neither is it fickle. Each disciple knows where Jesus
stands. Each enemy reads honesty in his face. He plays no
language games. He tells those who have ears to hear what
is necessary for salvation. If we keep an eye on Christ, we
will be able to handle the obstacles the world or the flesh
or the devil fling in our path to prevent spiritual maturity.

Balance between everyday work and play happens
when we make space in our day for the Lord. Imbalance is
bound to occur if we focus on work only without recreation or on play only without the labor of love.

The same principle applies to persons and things. We
have to see them in their proper order and relationship to
God. Lacking this inner stance of obedience to the divine
will, we become victims of worldly pleasures and ambi-
tions. That is why letting go of external possessions is not
enough; we must let go of interior attachments, too.

Christ says that to follow him we must be ready to
leave mother, father, brothers, and sisters (cf. Mark
10:28–30). This is like saying that to enter the land of
mature intimacy, we must be willing to venture into

hitherto unexplored regions of form-reception ("Whither shall I go, Lord?") and form-donation ("What would you have me do, Lord?").

## FACILITATING CONDITIONS FOR CHRISTIAN MATURITY

On this road we need the company of three stalwart dispositions of the heart. These are *humility* (self-accepting truth); *charity* (self-donating love); and *detachment* (self-relinquishing liberation).

Progress in spiritual maturity comes to a halt if we do not resist vain reasoning and defensive postures. We have to be willing to help other people with the gifts God has given us, even if this means bearing with dishonor, ridicule, and misunderstanding for Christ's sake.

These three conditions for spiritual maturation are essential according to the spiritual counsels given by St. Teresa of Avila in her book, *The Way of Perfection*. She calls humility the "queen" of the virtues, insisting that it means to walk in the truth of who we are and to be content with whatever it is the Lord wants us to do.

Bearing our crosses bravely as Jesus did is for her a trustworthy indicator that we are growing in humility. This is her way of saying that our intimacy with God, self, and others is ripening on the vine of redeeming love.

We cross new hurdles every time our own spiritual growth serves the good of others. Such is the case when we practice social justice, peace, and mercy; when we show compassion for our own and others' vulnerability; when we make Christ the center of our life while reaching out to others in his name.

St. Teresa assures us that if we are humble, charitable, and detached, then we shall find ourselves on the way to a happy and fulfilling life. She tells us that humility, detachment, and charity constitute a trinity of virtues modeled on the Triune God and embodied fully in Jesus. He is the humble, detached, charitable person we ought to emulate—whether life asks us to meet the demands of ministry or to seek repletion in solitude and prayer.

## MODELING OUR MATURITY ON THE LIFE OF MARY

What if our mission in life makes the headlines? What if we remain hidden in an ordinary household? In either case the way to become spiritually mature remains the same: we must be true to our call in the public as well as in the private sphere. There is a special person to whom we can turn to help. She is a model of humility, detachment, and charity. She is Mary, our mother in faith. Her story inspires our search.

Prior to the miracle of the Annunciation, we can imagine Mary's faith-filled life of devotion. She trusted God totally and had only one desire: to obey God's will. She awaited the Messiah, fully confident that he would fulfill the promises conveyed to the chosen people through scripture and tradition.

When Mary heard the angel's voice and gave her consent to be the mother of God, in her humanness she felt genuinely disturbed ("How could this be?"), yet she did not falter for a moment. She made a leap of faith and through her cooperation the Word became flesh and dwelt among us (cf. John 1:14).

For us, too, to follow the way of mature intimacy with God entails a rupture of complacency. We need to turn our life over to God, to make a fresh start. None of us can foresee in detail the implications of our response. We must strive, as Mary did, to be faithful to the divine plan even if its outcome in our lives is not clear.

Nothing could dissuade Mary from her free choice to surrender. By the time she visited her cousin Elizabeth, she felt exultant (cf. Luke 1:39–55). She wanted to share her good news. She greeted Elizabeth with a jubilant outburst of joy, declaring herself to be the lowly servant of the Lord.

Throughout the nativity narratives, it is apparent that Christ, born of Mary, is born anew in each of us. Our journey in faith, like Mary's, has to pass beyond the initial stage of elation. Events like the flight into Egypt (cf. Matt. 2:13–15) and the presentation of Jesus in the temple, when Simeon warned Mary that a sword would pierce her heart (cf. Luke 2:34–35), signal a new stage of spiritual deepening, one that includes sorrow and crushing reminders of life's limits.

The reins of control slip out of our hands as God's mysterious plan unfolds. When does life anyway proceed according to our expectations? God's ways are beyond what human minds can fathom. We simply trust that a higher meaning will be revealed to us in due course. In the meantime, as Mary did, so must we wait upon the word of the Lord with patient endurance and gentle relinquishment of how things should be. What is, is. Spirituality requires a good dose of reality to remain on course. Desert experiences lead us to deeper ranges of divine intimacy.

Think of Mary when Jesus left the coziness of their Nazareth home to begin his public ministry. She, like all mothers, had to let go of her usual routines—things like preparing his favorite foods, seeing that he had the proper clothes and a warm place to sleep. How broken-hearted she must have felt at the foot of the cross. How stark the pain of her powerlessness! Yet she had this teaching of his to console her heart: unless a grain of wheat goes underground and dies, it cannot bring forth good fruit (cf. John 13:24).

At supreme moments of poverty, God may clarify our mission. Consider what happened to Mary. In her lowliness she was given the highest place in the history of salvation. In her meekness she attained the fullness of spiritual maturity. Through the practice of everyday intimacy in the holy family, she became a vessel of faith, hope, and love. In her virginity motherhood paradoxically found its fullest meaning.

Spiritual maturity calls for a willingness on our part to be radically transformed. Only when we die with Christ can we rise with him to glory. Only then can God channel through our weakness saving nourishment to a world hungering not only for physical sustenance and emotional security but for spiritual depth.

Married or single, actively involved or quietly secluded, we become who we are meant to be by becoming the humble, charitable, detached, receptive, self-giving, and serene persons God intended us to be from the beginning.

The example of Mary shows us that new life takes root at the foot of the cross. The stages of deepening we witness in her life—from consolation to desolation to transformation—are essential starting points on the way to spiritual maturity and to the fullness of peace and joy only Christ can give.

Lord, in your unprecedented generosity
You raised our nothingness to nobility.
Lead me beyond the need for elation
To a consistent commitment to donation.
When a sword pierces my heart,
Let me feel a part of Mary's maturation
In detachment, charity, and humility,
For she trusted you totally
And grew daily in mature intimacy.
Shatter my complacency,
Heal my scarred emotionality
That I may learn to love unselfishly.
Let me relinquish my expectations
Of what might be
The outcome of creative ministry.
Buoyed by hope, let me explore
The deeper ranges of divine intimacy.
Grant me the grace of holy equanimity
Until I arrive, a pilgrim at your door.

# ✦ 12 ✦

# Recovering Freedom for Intimacy

THERE WAS SOME ONE THING THAT WAS TOO GREAT
FOR GOD TO SHOW US WHEN HE WALKED UPON OUR
EARTH; I HAVE SOMETIMES FANCIED IT WAS HIS
MIRTH.

—G. K. Chesterton

Like people gathered around the hearth on a cold night, we long to huddle together in the warm circle of recovered intimacy. We don't want to be like strangers in a foreign land. Where do we belong? The answer is nowhere without the Lord. "Make your home in me, as I make mine in you" (John 15:4). This is his ever-welcoming invitation to wandering hearts.

To foster the recovery of intimacy, we must abandon ourselves to the Mystery. How else can we take in stride the misunderstanding, the feelings of loneliness and rejection, the inescapable sickness and suffering we must all endure from time to time? Whether we are rich or poor, young or old, healthy or infirm, we can be givers and receivers of Christ's love.

Once we walk the way of mature intimacy with Jesus, we start to change. Not only does courtesy become second nature to us; conflict also seems easier to bear. Rather than being an obstacle it becomes a companion on the way to recovered intimacy. No happy ending could come to pass without it.

## CONFLICT AS A COLLISION COURSE

Conflict would appear to be anything but a conduit to intimacy. The flare-ups between people can simmer and explode like ancient feuds. Stress makes us feel as if our very bones are in rebellion. Peace of mind disappears like a brook scorched by the sun.

Life in conflict is like a tug of war—part of us knows what our faith teaches about patience, love, forgiveness, generosity; part of us pulls away. The good that I would do, I do not and the evil that I would not do, that I do (cf. Rom. 7:19). Paul's struggle becomes our own.

The worst conflicts invariably take place on the highest levels of our life. Nothing depletes felt intimacy faster than spiritual aridity. So devastating can such conflicts be that we may even doubt the efficacy of our calling. Joy becomes a distant memory. Like the man Job we may sink into a kind of low-grade depression.

Our body signals conflict before our mind accepts it as real. Signs of a conflicted self may range from inexplicable aches and pains to an elevation of blood pressure to a period of exhausting insomnia. The people closest to us aggravate us the most. Irritation and anger can erode trustworthy intimacy. We can't seem to shake off the nagging spirits that shadow us.

Our self-perception also suffers. We may experience self-doubt, disgust, or despair. Our perception of God changes, too. We may feel utterly sinful and unworthy of forgiveness. Inwardly and outwardly things are a mess.

When such conflicts tighten their grip, the pain can be devastating. Our physical and spiritual life is in shambles. We feel like a scattered puzzle. Can conflict be a positive force or is it always negative? Is it a companion on the way or an enemy?

## CONFLICT AS CREATIVE

Life shows us that there is no way to escape conflict as long as we are alive. The calm precedes a storm.

Disagreements among family and community members are normal occurrences, to say nothing of the pushes and pulls we have to put up with in our own personality. The clouds of conflict do have a silver lining. Conflict can evoke the self-directive questions we must ask if we want to stave off pseudo-intimacy and mature in the Lord.

Conflict cannot be ignored as inconsequential. It always means something. That meaning will haunt us unless we are willing to explore it. Conflict can be creative. It can result in our making a stronger commitment to Christ, but this does not happen overnight.

## FACING ISSUES COURAGEOUSLY

Conflict forces us to admit that something is wrong. Is it that our expectations have not been met? That our relationships are not fulfilling? That our job is unsatisfactory?

That our spiritual life is lukewarm? The facile solution to conflict—to escape it—has to be resisted. Dissonance cannot be obliterated like chalk dust on a wet board. It serves our quest for deeper consonance and a return to ordinary intimacy.

Conflict releases both depreciative and appreciative forces. On the one hand, we may be bombarded by fear, resentment, anger, and frustration. Tap us and you release a veritable volcano of conflicts and complaints. Held in too long or not harnessed for a higher purpose, this negative energy will explode. The challenge before us is to make dissonance an opening to deeper consonance and restored intimacy with God, self, and others. How does this turn for the better occur?

Rather than try to resolve these issues alone, it is wise to go for help to a trusted other. Part of the problem may be that we have been walking on the thin ice of self-sufficiency instead of seeking the shore of intimate sharing.

Up to now we may have resisted conflict, as if it were an alien force, instead of embracing it as a call to further freedom. With the proper encouragement, we can face into the center of the storm. This time of physical, emotional, and spiritual turmoil is also a time of grace. It prompts us to depend on God with the humility and courage Christ displayed in his darkest hour.

Conflict has immense formative potential, provided we channel its energy properly. With the eyes of faith, it can be seen as a formation opportunity. "Breakthroughs" may only happen when something in or around us "breaks down." For example, a couple seeks marriage counseling because of stress that has been eroding real intimacy. An addicted person goes to an Alcoholics

Anonymous (AA) meeting because he or she has hit rock bottom. An elderly man returns to some semblance of independent living only after his son and daughter-in-law move to another city.

Conflict becomes an avenue to creativity and restored intimacy when we use it to reexamine our life direction. Conflict compels us to reappraise if we are using or refusing our gifts.

Just as Jacob wrestled with the angel until he received an answer (cf. Gen. 32:23–33), so our times of wrestling with God can initiate honest, soul-searching exchanges. We pray best with wounded hearts. Such prayers of pure faith ascend to the ear of the Lord with lightning speed:

> Hear my cry, O God.
>> listen to my prayer!
> From the brink of Sheol I call;
>> my heart grows faint.
> Raise me up, set me on a rock.
>> for you are my refuge,
>> a tower of strength against the foe.
> Then I will ever dwell in your tent,
>> take refuge in the shelter of your wings.
>> (Ps. 61:2–5)

Conflict can be the fuel that powers our flight to new visions and resolutions, depending on whether we see it as a danger or as an opportunity.

Once we accept conflict as a companion of ordinary intimacy, we can drop our stubborn ways and start to count our blessings. Conflict, lived creatively, builds character. It puts flesh on the bones of our desire to follow God's providential direction in our life. It redeems us from superficiality and makes us people of depth. We are graced with a clearer view of what God has in mind for us, for when the storm subsides, the ebb and flow of the sea become apparent.

Conflict, like cool rain, clears away the fog that obscures the inner glow of our divine life call. By shaking us loose from complacency, it releases the creative forces of renewed faith, hope, and love. It leads us to a level of consonance and Christlike trust hitherto unknown.

This connection between conflict and creativity can best be understood as a sharing in the dying and rising of Jesus. It is impossible to grow in intimacy with the Lord and others without going through a similar process.

## INTIMACY IN IMITATION OF CHRIST

Conflict brings us to the threshold of choice. It serves, rather than retards, the recovery of intimacy. Conflict pulverizes the myth that we can make it alone. What choice does misery have but to ask for mercy? Conflict enables us to put on the Lord Jesus Christ (cf. Rom. 13:14), as St. Augustine did. It challenges us to confront the subtle resistances to grace that keep loving intimacy at bay. It teaches us not self-reliance but reliance on God (cf. 1 Cor. 4:10).

The grace of God enables us to endure, to run the race to the finish, to keep the faith (cf. Tim. 4:7). The unspeakable brutality of the cross is not an end but a beginning. Any life call put to the test of conflict can make a new start if Christ is in the picture.

For Simeon the time of anxious waiting subsided when he held the infant Jesus in his arms (cf. Luke 2:27–32). For Mary Magdalene sorrow turned to joy when she told the disciples that Christ was risen (cf. Mark 16:1–8). The intense pain Peter felt because he betrayed Jesus (cf. John 18:25–27) paled in comparison with the intensity of his proclamation of love for the Lord (cf. John 21:15–17).

The power of faith prevails over the conflicts that keep us from proclaiming the good news. Conflict is thus a servant source of formation, a small price to pay for the freedom to follow our call.

## WAYS OF PRAYERFUL INTIMACY

Intimacy's recovery comes to its fullness in the life of prayer. We cannot force its advance. We must be patient. It takes time to learn how to follow the leading of the Spirit. It takes patience to listen to the still, small voice of the Triune God in the depths of our heart as well as in the demands of our world.

While pursuing the business of the day, we cannot ignore the Spirit-inspired nudges we feel to examine its ups and downs in a prayerful way: "Did I handle this difficult situation as Christ might have done? In what way did my decisions affect others? Did I act out of love for God and them or only for my own gratification?"

Allowing God to be as much a part of our ruminations as an intimate friend draws us to deeper union. At the start of the day we ask God for guidance. At the end of the day we replay the tape to see if we have or have not responded wisely. When distractions tap like raindrops against the windowpanes of our mind, we renew our attention and turn toward the Holy. In due time we may experience a deeper calm, a miracle of grace, words fail to convey.

Conflicts rise and fall while prayer flows ceaselessly on (cf. 1 Thess. 5:16–18). Through the power of grace we remain in the presence of the living God. Quiet concentration as well as ardent perseverance become lasting dispositions of our heart.

Intimacy with the Holy, experienced against the horizon of everyday work and play, becomes the underlying motif of our life. In its splendid ordinariness, it is like the air we breathe or the water that quenches our thirst. Dry spells of deprivation give way to oases of peace and joy, indescribable in their intimacy.

Old customs light up with new meaning. Revelation becomes celebration as the words of Scripture heard in our daily reading and in the liturgy disclose dimensions of our faith unseen until now. A word strikes us as if it were meant by God just for us. We treasure it in our heart because it represents a contact point between us and God, a place of grace, where we enjoy the intimate companionship of Christ.

At many unscheduled moments during the day—waiting at a traffic light, standing in line at a checkout counter, sitting in a doctor's office—we take time to recall the words of Scripture and the masters. They are like fragrant oil that saturates our soul.

We may not feel the effects of recovered intimacy right away, but just wait. There is a residue of consolation that carries us through deserts of desolation. In due time God will show us the meaning of these momentary illuminations, these brief glimpses, these passing but real experiences of a Presence beyond words that permeates our everyday existence.

Such moments of nearness may be fleeting but their impact is lasting. The gift of recovered intimacy long sought is now being delivered to our door.

Lord, draw me into the circle
Of intimacy you knew
In your childhood home,
The warmth that strengthened you
To stand alone.
Let my wandering heart
Become a part of your family,
In communion with the Blessed Trinity.
You accepted conflict
As a companion on the way.
It did not hinder the dawning
Of a new day, bright
With the efficacy of grace.
Halt in me the forces that erode
Intimacy's recovery. Transform me
From within that I may always shun sin.
When I walk on the thin ice
Of self-sufficiency, remind me to seek
The graciousness of your wounded face
So full of love and mercy.
Make my commitment to you,
Alone and in community,
Signal a new era of Christian unity,
A time of peace and consonance
Beyond the temporary dominance
Of deep unrest.
Put my love to the test of trustworthy intimacy.
Let it be a tribute to your goodness,
Truth and beauty.

# Conclusion

I know from experience that it is tempting to equate the life of the spirit with an occasional prayer muttered in the morning as I head into the fast lane. Work and its demands soon take precedence over worship. Action replaces contemplation instead of flowing from it. I am in danger of leading a kind of split existence, separating prayer times on Sunday from calls on Monday to publish, research, speak, and teach. The great challenge is not to sever work from worship but to bring these two realms of reality into friendly conversation.

At a time when people hunger for spirituality, we know that intimacy with God cannot be a luxury reserved only for Christian mystics or acknowledged spiritual masters. It is a survival measure in the modern world. It belongs in the marketplace. It is the glue that holds everything else together. It is the life blood that makes us distinctively human, not animals or robots, but whole and holy persons.

I believe that true spirituality—not its here-today-gone-tomorrow new-age version—is the center out of which we must live if we are to execute efficiently the plans and projects entrusted by God to our care.

Competence and functional performance are not meant to be ends in themselves but expressions of our faith in God, our love for humankind. We see evidence everywhere of the depletion of values in family life and in the marketplace. Ethical behavior seems to have become a "throw-away commodity," even for many educated and skilled professionals. A lack of dedication affects everything from classroom teaching to appliance repair. To address these problems corporate executives enter into a dialogue with university administrators to foster management-style efficiency. Seminars on business and medical ethics proliferate. Books on values roll off the presses.

Laudable as all of these efforts are, the question still remains: How do we connect abstract information about the virtuous life to the lived spiritual commitments that motivate people always to do what is right and to give of themselves? What would it take to convince young and old alike never to lie, cheat, or steal merely to get ahead in private or public life? The answer lies not in inventing new technology but in fostering deep transformation of heart.

The shift from individualistic calculation to intimate sharing, from selfishness to charity, cannot happen unless we learn to integrate prayer and service, meditation and the demands of the marketplace. A good starting point is to engage as time allows in the practice of reflective reading of the Scriptures and the spiritual classics in a slowed-down, thoughtful way—a way that draws us into an intimate relationship with such giants as of the spiritual life as Augustine of Hippo, the fourth-century bishop whose teachings enabled the church to survive the barbarism of the Dark Ages; Catherine of Siena, a lay woman who, in the fourteenth century, found herself called upon to advise the papacy; Søren Kierkegaard, who in the nineteenth century declared himself to be a "spy for the Eternal" while moving philosophy into the modern age; and Dietrich Bonhoeffer, who gave his life during the Nazi purge rather than compromise his beliefs. In surveying the books of these and other masters, we find common themes that pertain to the integration of intimacy and ordinary living.

> 1. The first is *longing*. Spiritual seekers long for God as thirsty travelers long for a cool drink. They are not satisfied with a lukewarm or Sunday-only excuse for spirituality. They know that no matter how much we accomplish, our hearts, to cite Augustine, are restless until they rest in God. There is in us an unvoiced yearning that can be put on the backburner, but it is not likely to go away.

I remember feeling just such a longing. It happened of all places at Spaceport USA in Florida. I was viewing an IMAX film, entitled *The Dream Is Alive*, on a five-story-high screen. The film was especially poignant because several of the astronauts who died in the Challenger tragedy were part of the Discovery mission on which this film was based. Seeing on an immense screen some of the most dramatic photos ever made of our planet, I could not help but experience a sudden longing to be united with the mystery that pervades cosmos and creation. Did this same longing draw the brave souls of the Discovery crew to risk everything to follow their dream? Their decision to explore outer space signified to me a mark of that distinctively human or spiritual quality that enables human beings to see beyond problems to creative solutions, beyond dead ends to new openings.

> 2. A second theme involves *knowing who we are*. This is an essential dictum of the spiritual life. How can we discover what we are to do with our gifts and talents, how we are to use them for the common good, if we don't know who we are? Self-knowledge is also a key to intimacy. It enables us to acknowledge our limits while disclosing new potentials. It teaches us the wisdom of humility. Pride cut off from our dependency on God prevents us from seeing deeper truths. To Teresa of Avila, humility was a matter of walking in the truth of who we are. It teaches us to rely less on the shaky soil of egocentric projects and more on the solid ground of intimate, Christ-centered prayer. Humility is the spark that lights the fire of creative projects devoted to caring for others in self-detachment and charity.

It was wonderful to watch as each astronaut, with his or her gifts and talents, coalesced to form a team of professionals. It was clear from the start of the mission to its successful touchdown that these people knew who they were and what they were doing. They respected and complemented one another. They took pride in their mission but not at the expense of any one person. They could even tease one another and maintain good humor in tense situations.

It is striking to note that the words *humility* and *humor* share the same roots—the Latin word *humus*, meaning soil or ground. To be humble and to accomplish with God's grace great things is to maintain one's humor. It is to remember that in the end we are only "humans"— but how beautiful "dirt" can be as we behold from the dark vastness of outer space the fragile beauty of this planet made from of soil and fire, water and wind, this spaceship Earth we call our home.

> 3. The third theme is *love*. It is impossible to connect the inner journey to outer accomplishments unless we are motivated not by self-gain but by love for God and neighbor. Love is not a shallow self-centered emotion; it has to be expressed in good works. Love is the link between union with God and communion with those entrusted to our care in daily life. God's self-gift to us has to be expressed in the unsparing gift of ourselves to others. Love sets us free from the bonds of selfishness. It prompts us to dedicated service in home and society. Without love, friendship and family life fall apart. That is why we need ordinary intimacy to rebuild our society.

Returning to the film for a moment, it was clear as the mission unfolded that everyone involved in it, from the technicians in Houston to the crew itself, did what they were doing out of love for the task at hand and the felt conviction that their work would make a difference. Their witness of dedication is one we cannot emphasize enough in today's world. We need to restore the bond between love and work lest the quality of life remain in decline.

Recent studies show—and common sense tells us—that something has to be done to reverse the downward pulls destroying our world. Urban areas are aging; the wilderness is being eroded; modes of transportation are not as efficiently run as they ought to be; violence has turned our streets into killing fields. Unless we are oblivious to reality, we can see that few have a passion for justice, peace, and mercy. Greed peels away generosity; avarice replaces altruism; competitiveness cancels out collegiality. If we are to keep the dream alive, we must foster the freedom for intimacy that makes everyday work and play a true celebration of the human spirit.

These three themes—longing for God, growing in self-knowledge through humility, and integrating love and service to others—are basic conditions for living an intimately integrated prayerful and professional life. Such values are not meant to remain mere ideals or abstractions; they need to be embodied in our schools, churches, hospitals, family gatherings, and boardrooms.

Longing is connected with awe and wonder, with hope in the face of apparent hopelessness, with the graced awareness that we have gotten through an impossible challenge and survived.

Similarly, self-knowledge is not a definition we find in learned treatises or on a personality inventory. It is the outcome of lived experiences of success and failure, blessings and burdens. It is a recognition that hits us when we look in the mirror one day and wonder what we have been doing with our life. It gels when we take a "holy pause" to reflect on where we are going and why. To walk

LATE HAVE I LOVED THEE

in the truth is no easy thing, but only when we do so does life begin to take on new meaning.

Love is inseparable from service, generosity from justice, freedom from discipline. Love unfortunately is an overused word. It is, some say, a fuzzy feeling or a fun time. But love is more than a puppy or a party. It is the force that motivates us to give of our best self, to make sacrifices for our family, to spend an extra moment with a sick friend, to reach into our pockets for the poor. It flows like an energy current through a room when we treat people decently and assure them of our concern.

The diseases of sexism and racism, of narcissism and hedonism, erode the intimate bent of the human spirit and interject into this beautiful world of ours a climate of disease. Maybe the entire human organism at this moment of time needs to consult the Divine Physician, who alone can shake us out of the stupor of self-centeredness and set our hearts on fire with love. Cost-effectiveness will not be overlooked, but neither will the awareness that both what we do and how much we earn must serve a higher purpose. It must in some way serve the good of all or everyone on earth will be a loser.

I hope this book has both sobered your assessment of where we are and helped you to move beyond the mire of gloom and doom that cramp our freedom for intimacy. The turn of this century marks the return of a profound era of spiritual renewal calling for personal and social transformation. The intimacy with God, self, and others we seek cannot be rooted in human effort alone; it must well up from within through the action of grace and the gift of our humble response to it.

128

# Select Bibliography

Aelred of Rivaulx. *On Spiritual Friendship.* Trans. Mary Eugenia Laker. Washington, D.C.: Cistercian Publications, 1974.

de Saint Exupéry, Antoine. *Flight to Arras.* Trans. Lewis Galantiére. Alexandria, Va.: Time-Life, 1991.

Augustine, Saint. *Confessions.* Trans. Vernon J. Bourke. Washington, D.C.: The Catholic University of America Press, 1953.

Bernard of Clairvaux. *Sermons on the Song of Songs.* Trans. Killian Walsh. Cistercian Fathers Series: No. 4. Kalamazoo, Mich.: Cistercian Publications, 1971.

Catherine of Siena, St. *The Dialogue of Catherine of Siena.* Trans. Suzanne Noffke, O.P. Classics of Western Spirituality. New York: Paulist Press, 1980.

Ciszek, Walter with Daniel L. Flaherty. *He Leadeth Me.* New York: Doubleday, 1975.

Edwards, Tilden. *Living Simply through the Day: Spiritual Survival in a Complex Age.* New York: Paulist Press, 1977.

Francis, St., and St. Clare. *Francis and Clare: The Complete Works.* Trans. Regis Armstrong and Ignatius Brady. Classics of Western Spirituality. New York: Paulist, 1982.

Francis de Sales and Jane de Chantal. *Letters of Spiritual Direction.* Trans. Péronne Marie Thibert. Classics of Western Spirituality. New York: Paulist, 1988.

John of the Cross. *The Collected Works.* Trans. Kieran Kavanaugh and Otilio Rodriguez. Washington, D.C.: Institute of Carmelite Studies, 1991.

Kierkegaard, Søren. *Purity of Heart Is to Will One Thing: Spiritual Preparation for the Office of Confession.* Trans. Douglas V. Steere. New York: Harper, 1956.

Lawrence of the Resurrection, Brother. *The Practice of the Presence of God.* Trans. Donald Attwater. Springfield, Ill.: Templegate, 1974.

Lindberg, Anne. *Gift from the Sea.* New York: Pantheon, 1955.

Maloney, George A. *Called to Intimacy.* New York: Alba House, 1983.

Celeste, Sr. Marie. *The Intimate Friendships of Elizabeth Ann Bayley Seton.* New York: Alba House, 1989.

Muto, Susan. *Approaching the Sacred: An Introduction to Spiritual Reading.* Denville, N.J.: Dimension Books, 1973.

———. *Blessings that Make Us Be: A Formative Approach to Living the Beatitudes.* New York: Crossroad; Reprinted Petersham, Mass.: St. Bede's, 1980.

———. *Celebrating the Single Life: A Spirituality for Single Persons in Today's World.* New York: Crossroad, 1982.

———. *John of the Cross for Today: The Ascent.* Notre Dame, Ind.: Ave Maria Press, 1991.

———. *John of the Cross for Today: The Dark Night.* Notre Dame, Ind.: Ave Maria Press, 1994.

———. *The Journey Homeward: On the Road of Spiritual Reading.* Denville, N.J.: Dimension Books, 1977.

———. *Meditation in Motion.* New York: Doubleday, 1986.

———. *Pathways of Spiritual Living.* New York: Doubleday; Reprinted Petersham, Mass.: St. Bede's Publications, 1988.

———. *A Practical Guide to Spiritual Reading.* Petersham, Mass.: St. Bede's, 1994.

———. *Renewed at Each Awakening: The Formative Power of Sacred Words.* Denville, N.J.: Dimension Books, 1979.

———. *Steps Along the Way: The Path of Spiritual Reading.* Denville, N.J.: Dimension Books, 1976.

———. *Womanspirit: Reclaiming the Deep Feminine in Our Human Spirituality.* New York: Crossroad, 1991.

————— and Adrian van Kaam. *Commitment: Key to Christian Maturity*. Mahwah, N.J.: Paulist Press, 1989.

————— and Adrian van Kaam. *Commitment: Key to Christian Maturity. A Workbook and Guide*. Mahwah, N.J.: Paulist Press, 1991.

————— and Adrian van Kaam. *Divine Guidance: Seeking to Find and Follow the Will of God*. Ann Arbor, Mich.: Servant, 1994.

————— and Adrian van Kaam. *Stress and the Search for Happiness*. Williston Park, N.Y.: Resurrection Press, 1993.

————— and Adrian van Kaam. *Harnessing Stress*. Williston Park, N.Y.: Resurrection Press, 1994.

————— and Adrian van Kaam. *Healthy and Holy Under Stress*. Williston Park, N.Y.: Resurrection Press, 1994.

Polcio, Anna, ed. *Intimacy: Issues of Emotional Living in an Age of Stress for Clergy and Religious*. Whitinsville, Mass.: Affirmation Books, 1978.

Rubin, Lillian B. *Intimate Strangers: Men and Women Together*. New York: Harper & Row Perennial Library, 1983.

Stevens, Clifford, J. *Intimacy with God: Notes on the Vocation to Celibacy*. Schuyler, Neb.: BMH Publications, 1992.

Storms, Kathleen. *Simplicity of Life as Lived in the Everyday*. Washington, D.C.: University of America Press, 1983.

Teresa of Avila. *The Interior Castle*. Trans. Kieran Kavanaugh and Otilio Rodriguez. Classics of Western Spirituality. New York: Paulist Press, 1979.

Teresa of Avila. *The Way of Perfection in The Collected Works of St. Teresa of Avila*. Vol. Two. Trans. Kieran Kavanaugh and Otilio Rodriguez. Washington, D.C.: Institute of Carmelite Studies, 1980.

Thérèse of Lisieux. *Collected Letters of St. Thérèse of Lisieux*. Trans. F. J. Sheed. Westminster, Md.: Christian Classics, 1974.

Tyrrell, Thomas J. *Urgent Longings: Reflections on Infatuation, Intimacy, Sublime Love*. Mystic, Conn.: Twenty-Third Publications, 1994.

Underhill, Evelyn. *Practical Mysticism*. New York: E. P. Dutton & Co., 1943.

van Kaam, Adrian. *In Search of Spiritual Identity*. Denville, N.J.: Dimension Books, 1975.

————. *Dynamics of Spiritual Self-Direction*. Pittsburgh, Pa.: Epiphany Association, 1992.

————. *Looking for Jesus*. Denville, N.J.: Dimension Books, 1978.

————. *The Music of Eternity: Everyday Sounds of Fidelity*. Notre Dame, Ind.: Ave Maria Press, 1990.

————. *The Mystery of Transforming Love*. Denville, N.J.: Dimension Books, 1982.

————. *On Being Involved: The Rhythm of Involvement and Detachment in Human Life*. Denville, N.J.: Dimension Books, 1970.

————. *The Roots of Christian Joy*. Denville, N.J.: Dimension Books, 1985.

————. *Spirituality and the Gentle Life*. Pittsburgh, Pa.: Epiphany Books, 1994.

————. *The Vowed Life*. Denville, N.J.: Dimension Books, 1968.

————. *The Woman at the Well*. New Jersey: Dimension Books; Reprinted Pittsburgh, Pa.: Epiphany Books, 1993.

———— and Susan Muto. *Aging Gracefully*. Boston, Mass.: St. Paul Books, 1992.

———— and Susan Muto. *The Power of Appreciation*. New York: Crossroad, 1993.

———— and Susan Muto. *Practicing the Prayer of Presence*. Williston Park, N.Y.: Resurrection Press, 1993.

Vincent de Paul, St. *The Conferences of St. Vincent de Paul to the Sisters of Charity*. 4 Vols. Trans. Joseph Leonard. Westminster, Md.: Christian Classics, 1968.

Westley, Dick. *Redemptive Intimacy: A Perspective for the Journey to Adult Faith*. Mystic, Conn.: Twenty-Third Publications, 1981.